It Takes a Village to Raise a
SINGLE MOTHER

Agaytha B Corbin

WESTBOW
PRESS®
A DIVISION OF THOMAS NELSON
& ZONDERVAN

WestBow Press books may be ordered through booksellers or by contacting:

WestBow Press
A Division of Thomas Nelson & Zondervan
1663 Liberty Drive
Bloomington, IN 47403
www.westbowpress.com
844-714-3454

ISBN: 979-8-3850-2088-1 (sc)
ISBN: 979-8-3850-2089-8 (e)

Library of Congress Control Number: 2024904817

Print information available on the last page.

WestBow Press rev. date: 06/18/2024

CONTENTS

DEDICATION

This book is dedicated my parents, Ralph and Angerlener Corbin, my first village! I am honored to have been a Abraham and Sarah baby!

CHAPTER

"Thanks again for the ride, Katrina." I smiled at my best friend as I opened the passenger door and exited her car. Katrina also exited and opened the trunk of the car. The sun was shining brightly on the busy street with neat brick rows of apartments on either side.

"No problem at all," she smiled back. "Do you need help carrying the groceries to the house?"

"That's what I have these two strong handsome young men for," I motioned to my sons who were climbing out of the backseat of the car, gathering their book bags.

I divided up the bags of groceries between the three of us, and then said goodbye to Katrina before she waved and pulled away down the street.

"I'll be glad when we have our own car and don't have to ride the bus or ride with people." Desmond shifted his bags and squinted up at me.

"You know we should be thankful for the things we do have," I reminded my oldest son gently. "You remember the lady I was helping at work earlier?"

"I remember," Lamon piped up. "She was homeless and you helped her get food."

I nodded, surprised at how much the boys picked up while doing homework sitting in the room next to my office at the non-profit organization. The boys sometimes had to go with me after they got out of school to the office or to other community programs and events.

"At least she HAD a car," Desmond snapped back.

I was too tired to go back and forth about how hard it is to be living out of a car and how blessed we were even though we were barely getting by financially ourselves. My passion, the Community Development Corporation Resource Consortium, Incorporated, or CDCRC was a grassroots endeavor in west Dayton, Ohio with multiple sponsors. We encouraged financial literacy, networked small business development, and taught homebuyer education. By networking with business owners, local government, community leaders, and everyday people, the non-profit organization was a huge success. But it ran by the work of volunteers, and I sometimes made money through freelance consulting work.

"Let's go boys," I said, and we made our way up the sidewalk to our section of the apartments.

My open-door policy made way for meeting an interesting variety of people. The week before I had been invited to a business trip by Tim Caldwell, who flew my staff and I in his private jet to his private resort in Hilton Head, South Carolina. It was a lavish trip, complete with champagne and limousine rides. It was a very productive trip, and we laid the groundwork for another branch of the CDCRC called "Angel Auto," where we would network people with affordable transportation.

There was always so much work to be done, and time always flew by. But the strain

3

of having a limited income that depended on freelance work was taking its toll on my savings. Times had been financially tight since I broke up with my youngest son's father and moved from a house to this modest apartment with my sons. I sacrificed and went without in order to provide a comfortable life for my family.

As we trudged down the stairs to our floor, a white paper posted on my apartment door caught my eye. My heart sank knowing that it was an eviction notice that had been posted earlier that day. I knew it was coming, and I had prayed for more freelance work to help me cover the bills, but as I walked up and unlocked the door to our home I was overwhelmed and tears began to well up in the corners of my eyes.

I pushed the door open and set the grocery bags down on the dining room table. The boys sensed my sadness and were quiet as they put their bags on the table as well. I went back to the door and peeled the notice off the door, my eyes focused on "30 days to vacate the property." The words on the letter blurred together as tears clouded my eyes and began to fall down my cheeks. I closed and locked the door and walked over to the green sofa in our living room and sat down.

My mind raced with how to handle this situation. Who could I ask for help? If we moved, where would we go? I had stepped out in faith and given my full-time effort to make the non-profit organization what I felt God had put in my heart to accomplish. Why had he made a way for the success of the business but not for me and my sons?

The boys were silent because they rarely saw me crying and knew something had to be extremely wrong for me to be this upset.

"Mom," Desmond said softly. "What's wrong?" I couldn't answer. I just shook my head and reached for a tissue to dry my eyes.

Lamon grabbed the tissue box and handed me a Kleenex.

"It's going to be okay." He said as he put an arm around my shoulder.

I smiled through my tears at my sons and nodded. I had no words for them right then, for in my heart I was crying out to my heavenly Father for strength.

"I have done everything I can do to make things work for me and my boys." I prayed inwardly. "Show me what to do…"

It Takes a Village to Raise
A Single Mom
Agaytha Corbin's story

End of the Chapters Scriptures and Thoughts: Chapter (1) Decisions

A single mom's decisions: in my journey as a mother and in this chapter a new mother, I began to understand more clearly the impact of my decisions. There is always either a positive or negative impact from one's decision.

Here is a Biblical example of a woman making a decision, and how it impacted her life and many generations thereafter, both with negative and positive outcomes.

Let's talk about Eve, the original Mother and her decision to listen to the serpent and eat from the forbidden tree of Life that impacted the world.

Genesis 3:1-21 NIV

The Fall

1 Now the serpent was more crafty than any of the wild animals the Lord God had made. He said to the woman, "Did God really say, 'You must not eat from any tree in the garden'?"

2 The woman said to the serpent, "We may eat fruit from the trees in the garden,

3 But God did say, 'You must not eat fruit from the tree that is in the middle of the garden, and you must not touch it, or you will die.'"

4 "You will not certainly die," the serpent said to the woman.

5 "For God knows that when you eat from it your eyes will be opened, and you will be like God, knowing good and evil."

6 When the woman saw that the fruit of the tree was good for food and pleasing to the eye, and also desirable for gaining wisdom, she took some and ate it. She also gave some to her husband, who was with her, and he ate it.

7 Then the eyes of both of them were opened, and they realized they were naked; so they sewed fig leaves together and made coverings for themselves.

8 Then the man and his wife heard the sound of the Lord God as he was walking in the garden in the cool of the day, and they hid from the Lord God among the trees of the garden.

9 But the Lord God called to the man, "Where are you?"

10 He answered, "I heard you in the garden, and I was afraid because I was naked; so I hid."

11 And he said, "Who told you that you were naked? Have you eaten from the tree that I commanded you not to eat from?"

12 The man said, "The woman you put here with me—she gave me some fruit from the tree, and I ate it."

13 Then the Lord God said to the woman, "What is this you have done?" The woman said, "The serpent deceived me, and I ate."

14 So the Lord God said to the serpent, "Because you have done this, "Cursed are you above all livestock and all wild animals! You will crawl on your belly and you will eat dust all the days of your life.

15 And I will put enmity between you and the woman, and between your offspring and hers; he will crush your head, and you will strike his heel."

16 To the woman he said, "I will make your pains in childbearing very severe; with painful labor you will give birth to children. Your desire will be for your husband, and he will rule over you."

17 To Adam he said, "Because you listened to your wife and ate fruit from the tree about which I commanded you, 'You must not eat from it,' "Cursed is the ground because of you; through painful toil you will eat food from it all the days of your life.

18 It will produce thorns and thistles for you, and you will eat the plants of the field.

19 By the sweat of your brow you will eat your food until you return to the ground, since from it you were taken; for dust you are and to dust you will return."

20 Adam named his wife Eve, because she would become the mother of all the living.

21 The Lord God made garments of skin for Adam and his wife and clothed them.

22 And the Lord God said, "The man has now become like one of us, knowing good and evil. He must not be allowed to reach out his hand and take also from the tree of life and eat, and live forever."

23 So the Lord God banished him from the Garden of Eden to work the ground from which he had been taken.

24 After he drove the man out, he placed on the east side of the Garden of Eden cherubim and a flaming sword flashing back and forth to guard the way to the tree of life.

What was the <u>negative</u> impact of Eve's decision to eat the fruit at the forbidden tree of Life?

Example(s): Sin and death entered into the world. The pain of childbirth.

(1) _____

(2) _____

(3) _____

What was the <u>positive</u> impact of Eve's decision to eat the fruit at the forbidden tree of Life?

Example(s): The promise of a Redeemer being born to defeat the enemy-sin/death taken away by Him. The start of the family (Villages were created)

(1) _____

(2) _____

(3) _____

I recommend that as you read my story you journal on how your decisions as a single parent may have impacted you kids, your family, friends and life as a whole. And how God's grace still held it all together regardless of those decisions.

I testify in this book that my decision to have my sons was impactful to me, to my sons, to family and to their fathers. However, the impact of their lives being here living and being prosperous outweighed all the negative impacts of my decision. I decided to move forward as a single mother who loved her children and wanted the best for them despite my circumstances.

CHAPTER

TWO

"T hanks again for taking me to the clinic," Alicia said.

"Girl, it's no problem at all," I smiled at my best friend in the passenger seat.

"I don't know what I'm going to do if I am pregnant," Alicia sighed. "You know my momma gonna kill me if I end up knocked up before we finish all this college she paid for."

"Believe me, I know!" I shook my head as I watched the University of Cincinnati campus fade behind us in the rearview mirror.

"Oh man, this is my jam!" Alicia turned up the radio as Color Me Badd smoothly crooned in the background. "I wanna sex you up!" Alicia sang along as the New Jack Swing filled the car.

"That is your problem in the first place," I joked. "We wouldn't be riding to this clinic if you were being a good girl and keeping your head in those books instead of those boys."

"I know you ain't talking," Alicia laughed, and then looked at me seriously. "For real, you should take a pregnancy test too. You've been throwing up the last few mornings and please stop telling me it's a flu bug."

"It's nothing," I said, convinced that I was going to be fine after a few days.

"What if it is? Wouldn't you like to be sure?"

I watched as the flaming scarlet oak trees with their deep wine-colored foliage lining the street passed by. I thought of Chris, my ex-boyfriend and how he would react if I were pregnant. Also, my Father, Ralph Corbin. He would be so disappointed in his "little Peaches" if something like that were to offset my life plans.

I pushed these thoughts aside and focused on the road. It really wouldn't hurt to be sure about something as serious as being pregnant.

"Okay, you talked me into it. See what I get for coming with you to hold your hand? You can talk me into just about anything." I shook my head and glanced over at my best friend.

She didn't joke back with me. She was staring out the window watching the scenery and biting her neon pink thumbnail.

"Hey! It's going to be fine." I reassured her, putting my hand on her shoulder. "Best case scenario, it's nothing and you need to be more careful when you creeping. And worst-case scenario, it's a baby and we'll figure things out."

We were silent as we pulled into the parking lot of the clinic. A few minutes later we were inside sitting in the waiting room waiting to see the doctor. The fluorescent lights seemed dim and the worn tile floors smelled strongly of disinfectant. There was a couple sitting across from us in the shabby metal chairs, waiting to be called. They looked like they were married, in their early thirties, their faces seemed excited as they held hands and spoke to each other in hushed tones.

"The nurse will see you now," a receptionist called from her front desk and motioned for us to come forward. A nurse appeared through the double door beside the desk as we stood to follow her.

"You both are here together?" she asked

"Yes, and we both are getting a pregnancy test." I spoke up.

"Okay, follow me this way." The nurse led us through the doors and down a long corridor. She walked briskly and rambled about how beautiful the spring weather was before ushering us into a small room.

After drawing blood from both of us, we were led back to the waiting room where we again sat silently, waiting for the results and lost in thought.

An unexpected pregnancy although life-changing would not be the end of the world. I already knew that if the results came back positive, I would be keeping the baby. I, myself, had been an unexpected pregnancy. My parents Ralph and Angerlener Corbin had two grown sons and grandchildren when I came along. Our family village was in west Dayton, Ohio. Being born to parents who were older in years had its advantages. I grew up with my nephews and nieces who felt more like brothers and sisters because of our similar ages. The family affectionately called me "Peaches" because I was the peach of their eyes. Both of my parents were from the south: Dad was from Alabama and Mom was from Texas. They both had lived through the Great Depression and Dad had served in Europe in World War II. It was a part of our family values that all life was a gift from God and considered precious.

The married couple that had been waiting before we arrived had been called back for their results and it was just Alicia and I sitting in the lobby. I looked over at Alicia. She was leaning back in her seat staring at the ceiling. Her eyebrows were furrowed and her lips were pressed together in a thin line. I reached over for her hand just as the married couple came through the double doors. Alicia perked up and we watched the couple walk out of the lobby and out the front door. On their faces was the look of pure happiness and excitement as they held each other close. I could feel from the glow about them that they were completely ready to welcome a new life into their home.

"Agaytha Corbin!" the nurse called, jarring me back to my reality. "Come on back." I got up and followed her back to the room and made myself comfortable in the chair.

The nurse looked over her clipboard and then up at me. "The results are positive. You are pregnant."

The rest of what she said faded away as wave after wave of emotions engulfed me.

I knew I wasn't ready to be a parent and start a family. I knew it was going to be a big commitment and a great responsibility. And I knew I couldn't do it alone.

"If you are interested, we can make an appointment for you to terminate your pregnancy," the nurse voice came back into focus.

"No thank you," I said quickly. "I will be keeping my baby."

I found myself back in the lobby waiting for my best friend, my mind racing with all the things I needed to do. I had to tell Chris, the baby's father, what was going on. Chris and I grew up in the same neighborhood when we were 10 years old. I could tell he had a crush on me back then, but we started dating when we were grown after Frank, my nephew, re-introduced us at the University of Cincinnati campus. I loved Chris, he was a good man, but I was unsure of how much he would be on board with the pregnancy since our break up, and how our relationship would progress from this point.

My parents would be disappointed. I knew they would be supportive as would the rest of the family, but I knew that having children out of wedlock was not how I had been taught growing up. I remembered other unmarried women and teens when I was younger who had kids and the stigma of shame and embarrassment that people heaped on them as they shook their heads and gossiped.

I was also unsure of how it would affect my college education. I knew I wanted to finish college and it would be harder taking care of a kid while juggling work and studying.

Alicia walked through the door towards me. "Let's get out of here," she said.

I stood and followed her out to the car and we got inside.

"You were right," tears welled up in my eyes. "I'm pregnant." Saying it out loud felt almost unreal.

"Yeah, me too." Her face was blank.

"It's going to be okay," I tried to comfort her. "We can figure things out."

"I'm not having it," Alicia stopped me. "I made an appointment with the nurse to terminate the pregnancy."

"You're going to have the abortion?"

"I'm not ready for all this, I still have a life to live and school to finish. Plus, you know my boyfriend ain't staying around, and Momma would kill me."

I looked at her. She had thought things through as much as I had, but in her eyes, I could see that her mind was made up and there wasn't much I could say to change how she felt. I started the car and headed back to our dorm on campus. The whole ride home I tried to pitch scenarios where things would work out, but she shot them all down.

"I'm glad for you," she admitted. "You have a supportive family and Chris is a good guy, he'll be a good dad. My man is gonna be on to the next girl and my momma has told me my whole life she ain't gonna raise no more kids. I would be on my own living in the projects and getting food stamps. There is no upside for me. Right now, I need to finish college and have a degree so I can make more than minimum wage and have a decent life. Maybe down the road when I've made it I can have some kids with a man that will be there for me. Right now, is not that time."

As I watched the familiar sights of my hometown of Dayton, Ohio pan by my view basking in the early morning sunshine, from the passenger side of my dad's car, I reflected on the changes that had occurred in my life. I was living back at home with my parents and taking classes at the community college downtown. The transition had not been easy, and my parents Ralph and Angerlener Corbin, although disappointed, were extremely supportive. Dad took the news the hardest. He found it difficult to look me in the eyes or conversate with me outside of polite small talk. He was always there to give me a ride to school or my frequent doctor appointments, but the silence between us was deafening for me.

I had stayed at the University of Cincinnati for as long as I could, working as a bank teller and taking classes, although I did move off campus to a studio apartment. Chris was unsure that the baby was his at first, and didn't share the news with his family until some months later.

The brighter side of the pregnancy was feeling all the support from friends, family, and coworkers. Both my coworkers and college friends threw me baby showers in Cincinnati. Everything was going good until the bank cut back on tellers, and I lost my job. With no income, the bills snowballed until my sports car was repossessed by the bank that fired me.

I was overwhelmed. I was in way over my head, and had no idea which way to turn. Early that morning around 4 AM, I sat on the edge of my bed and in a flood of tears I cried out to God. I was beginning to feel the weight of how big of a responsibility having this baby was, and realizing I couldn't do it all by myself.

"I'm going to have to give this baby back to you, Lord" I prayed out loud.

A wave of peace washed over me. I felt God's presence there with me comforting my soul. I could feel him saying that everything would be okay and that he would guide me in the ways I should go. I knew what I needed to do. I got up and went to the laundry room where they had a payphone. I made a collect call home and my mother answered the phone.

"Hello?"

"Momma?" my voice cracked and I started crying again.

"What is it Peaches?"

"I'm coming home."

"We'll be there to pack you up Friday."

And just like that, my village was there.

The car slowed to a stop in front of the college building, bringing me back to the present. "Thanks Dad," I smiled at him while opening the door.

"You're welcome, Peaches." He gave a half smile back. "You need me to pick you up after class this afternoon?"

"Chris is picking me up and going with me to my doctor's appointment," I replied. "I'll see you later this evening. Love you!"

"Love you too," he still avoided eye contact.

I shut the car door and waddled up the sidewalk to the concrete, three story building. Walking was becoming more difficult, and not just because of my growing midsection. My legs and feet were starting to swell and moving in general was painful.

I entered the classroom and headed for my usual desk in the middle of the row, against the wall. It was always so awkward getting in and out of the old school desk chairs especially at my size. I would feel like the entire class was watching as I scooted and shuffled around trying to get somewhat comfortable. Everyone was always nice and helpful though. I felt like being actively involved in academic work cut back on the stress, and was a great outlet for my creativity. I felt like it was important to continue to pursue my educational goals, as did my family. My time at school flew by, and before I knew it, Chris was there to take me to my doctor's appointment.

Our ride there was mostly quiet with just the radio playing in the background. At the appointment, the doctor informed me that I had toxemia, or pre-eclampsia. All the swelling in my legs and feet was due to high blood pressure and that the baby had a high risk of being born premature. Because of the severity of the toxemia, my appointments were scheduled weekly to keep tabs on my high-risk pregnancy. Chris took interest and asked a few questions, and I could tell that he cared and was concerned.

On the ride home, I remembered that Chris had told his family about the baby a few weeks ago and I wondered how it had gone.

"How did your family take the big news," I asked.

"They took it well," he shrugged. "They said we should get married."

"How do you feel about getting married?" I glanced over in his direction.

"I'm not ready for all that right now," he looked back at me. "Let's just focus on the baby and take things from there."

I nodded in agreement. "Your family is coming to the baby shower cookout at my brother Frank's house this weekend, right?"

"Yes," Chris' face lit up. "They are looking forward to it actually."

"That's great!" We pulled up to my parents' house and Chris parked the car and got out to help me on the other side. "Thanks Chris. I really appreciate your support."

Chris took my hand and helped me to my feet. He smiled and nodded, then grabbed my bookbag from the floor and carried it as he helped me up the sidewalk to the house.

"You coming inside?" I invited him.

"I have to go," he shook his head. "I'll see everyone at the baby shower though."

"Okay," I held out my arms. "See you this weekend."

He gave me a small hug as my mom was opening the front door. He smiled at her and waved before walking back to his car.

"Thank you, Chris," mom waved back.

It Takes a Village to Raise
A Single Mom
Agaytha Corbin's story

**End of the Chapters Scriptures and Thoughts: Chapter (2)
Transition**

Definition of transition: the process or a period of changing from one state or condition to another.

In Chapter (2) my life changed from a young carefree college student to a pregnant single mother coming back home to my parents-back to the city that I did not want to return to as an adult. But God had other plans for me and my new little family. Change is hard but it is necessary. When you are responsible for another human being-my unborn child- who I decided to keep, love and give back to Abba. Transition with the help of my village. When I released my resistance to the transition to go back home, I knew accepting my life as a pregnant adult woman made me a better mother to be. However, I didn't prepare to have stress in this transition. The impact on transitioning to my new village was great.

Scriptures:

Esther Chapters 1-5 Esther transitioned to the palace.

Esther 2:8 NIV So it came to pass, when the king's commandment and his decree was heard, and when many maidens were gathered together unto Shushan the palace, to the custody of Hegai, that Esther was brought also unto the king's house, to the custody of Hegai, keeper of the women.

Negative Impact: _____

_____

Positive Impact:_____

_____

Ruth Chap 1-4 Ruth transitioned to another land/home with her family member

Ruth 1:16 KJV And Ruth said, Intreat me not to leave thee, or to return from following after thee: for whither thou goest, I will go; and where thou lodgest, I will lodge: thy people shall be my people, and thy God my God:

Negative Impact: _____

_____

Positive Impact:_____

_____

    Genesis Chapter 12:1-12 KJV Sarah transitioned to another land with her husband Abraham

    1 Now the Lord had said unto Abram, Get thee out of thy country, and from thy kindred, and from thy father's house, unto a land that I will shew thee:

    2 And I will make of thee a great nation, and I will bless thee, and make thy name great; and thou shalt be a blessing:

    3 And I will bless them that bless thee, and curse him that curseth thee: and in thee shall all families of the earth be blessed.

Negative Impact: _____

_____

Positive Impact:_____

_____

CHAPTER

THREE

CHAPTER

THREE

My firstborn son Desmond came into our family village five weeks premature on June 11th, 1993. His birth was completely unexpected. One moment Chris and I were sitting in the obstetrician's office for my weekly check-up, and the next we were heading for the hospital to have labor induced due to the severe toxemia I was experiencing.

My mom, Angerlener, was the biggest help and support as I found my footing in motherhood. I was still living at home in my old bedroom that I shared with my newborn son. Desmond was colicky, and his crying at all hours was a big adjustment especially to my older retired parents, but they never complained.

One Saturday morning, I woke up to the strong smell of coffee brewing in the kitchen. I glanced over at Desmond's crib and to my surprise he was sleeping soundly for once. I stretched and rolled out of bed, slid into my slippers and robe and trudged down the hall. My mother was in the kitchen by herself, preparing breakfast.

"Good morning, Mom!"

"Good morning, Peaches!" She greeted me. "You want some coffee?"

"Yes please," I yawned.

"Did you sleep good?" Mom grabbed a mug and poured me a cup of coffee.

"Pretty well," I nodded. "Desmond actually slept decently last night. He only woke up crying three times."

Mom smiled and handed me the cup of coffee. "Hopefully he sleeps well again tonight. We can't have you in church falling asleep during the service tomorrow from being too tired."

"The church mothers are going to have something to say regardless," I shook my head and sipped the hot beverage. The church mothers were the senior citizen women who were considered the pillars of the church congregation. They could be sweet and grandmotherly at times, and other times they could be gossipy and judgmental. I remembered when I was pregnant and had morning sickness at the church. One of the church mothers noticed and before the week was over half of the church assumed I was pregnant due to her gossiping. I had been a Sunday school teacher before going away to college, so a couple of the church mothers felt like I should stand up front during service and apologize publicly for my sin of fornication.

"Don't you worry about anything," mom put her hand on her hip. "We are going to church to hear the Word and to be fed spiritually. If someone wants to start some nonsense, Angerlener Corbin will shut it down."

I smiled and leaned against the counter. She absolutely had my back and would defend me. When they confronted her about a public apology she had told them I would not be doing that, and they were wrong for focusing on the young women while never bothering the young men involved.

"How are things with you and Chris," mom asked as she crossed her arms. "I haven't seen as much of him since you had the baby."

"Chris is Chris," I sighed. "I don't think he knows what he wants."

"I know things can be frustrating, but you have to promise me something, Agaytha." Mom looked at me very seriously. "No matter how bad things are between you and Chris, please never talk negatively about him to you son. As he grows older he'll have his own conflicts and issues with his dad. Kids don't need to grow up with your baggage and resentments too. Always take the high road."

"I don't talk bad about Chris," I started.

"I know you don't," she interrupted. "I just wanted to share some wisdom to make life easier for you in the long run." Mom continued to bustle around the kitchen putting the finishing touches on breakfast. She paused for a minute and looked up at me. "What was it that attracted you to Chris Dixon? He always did like you ever since you were kids, but you didn't give him the time of day until you were grown and in college."

Her question caught me off guard. I had not really considered in depth how or why we had ended up being a couple. "Well you know nephew Frank re-introduced us down at University of Cincinnati." My older brother, Frank Jr's son, Frank III was close to my age and growing up he was always around looking out for me. In some ways he felt like the younger protective brother I never had. "I guess we hit it off because we had so much familiarity and history."

"But were you in love with him?" Mom was standing next to me looking directly into my eyes.

"I do have love for Chris," I said slowly. "But we were not in love."

A wave of emotions washed over me as I remembered the last time I had been in love and how my first heartbreak occurred a few months before Chris and I started dating. My first love and I knew each other from my parent's church in my last years of high school before college. He went to Wright State University and we commuted the 45 minutes to an hour between Dayton and Cincinnati mostly on weekends and sometimes during the school week. Everything was dreamy in the beginning, he was tall, dark, and handsome, and we were the perfect match. I imagined us getting married and spending the rest of my life with this man I loved with all my heart, growing old and having a fairy tale romance.

But as time progressed the dream of us sharing forever together turned into a nightmare. The man I gave my everything to started to become distant. I realized that you can't make a man love or want you. Our break up was so destructive mentally and emotionally that I was open to any distraction that would take my mind off of the pain I was experiencing.

I stared at the bottom of my empty coffee cup as tears began to well up in the corners of my eyes. I put the cup down and quickly wiped my eyes.

"When I met your father, I didn't fall head over heels in love with him," my mother took my hand in hers. "I was a single mother, struggling to make ends meet for me and your brother, Frank Jr. I had just gone through a divorce and your dad had too, but finding love was the last thing on my mind. Ralph pursued me for years before I gave in to his persistence. He was not the type I was attracted to back then."

"He wore you down," I laughed. I remembered my parents recounting their love story on multiple occasions. The start of their village was due to the persistence of my dad. They had met at the Old DECI warehouse, before it became a part of the Wright-Patterson Air Force Base after World War II. Even though Ralph had a physically demanding and sometimes messy job, he always dressed sharply in a crisply pressed white button up shirt, slacks, and a fedora, which was in drastic contrast to his peers who dressed casually. He was laid back, quiet, and reserved, and he was highly respected by both his black and white co-workers and bosses. Ralph's kind and observant mannerisms didn't attract Angerlener at all, and she flatly turned him down every time he would ask her out to lunch or dinner.

"He did wear me down." Mom admitted. "After a few years I finally consented and we began courting. He would say to me 'You gonna be my wife,' and I would tell him 'No I am not!' But after more years of him bringing me lunches, helping me and my young son, and being a perfect gentleman, I grew to love him."

After they were married Angelina moved from Springfield, Ohio to their current home in the Residence Park neighborhood on Whitmore Avenue in west Dayton, Ohio. She had lost two babies that were stillborn in her first marriage, and they both really hoped to have a daughter. Instead they had a son, Bennie. As time went on it seemed that their two sons were all that God would gift them with, and so they opened their home to Foster children. They had a happy family and were excellent Foster parents, my mother even won awards for going above and beyond in her care for the children.

"It's a good thing you learned to love him," I teased. "Otherwise I wouldn't be here."

"You were a complete surprise," mom had a distant look in her eyes, as if in some ways she still couldn't believe it. "I'll never forget that day at the doctor's office. Your daddy and I were both retired and the doctor came in, talking about 'Congratulations Mr. and Mrs. Corbin! You're having a baby!' I thought he was joking. I told him, 'You better go back and check that again.' Your daddy was tickled pink, he was so happy. I was in disbelief; our boys were grown and we were already grandparents! We had prayed for the blessing of a daughter for so long, but God knows when and where to answer our requests when it is in the fulfillment of His will for our lives."

Her story brought fresh tears to my eyes. The miracle of life overwhelmed me at that moment. Again, I felt the weight of the responsibility of the life I had brought into the world. I knew I had the love and support of my village around me, but I wondered what God had in store for me and my search for love and how things would work out with Chris and myself.

My mom put her arms around me in a hug. I hugged her back and cried softly on her shoulder. We stood there for a few minutes in silent embrace until a shrill cry from down the hall interrupted our moment.

"The baby is awake," I slowly pulled away from my mom.

My mother put her hands on my face. "You have always been a free-spirit, Peaches." I noticed the tears were running down my mother's face as well. "There is nothing wrong with that, just not everyone knows how to deal with it. Your father and I have tried to give you a happy life, and we might have spoiled you more than a little. You still have a lot of learning and growing to do. But I do think that having this baby is going to ground you."

I wasn't completely sure what she meant, but I smiled and hugged my mom again before going to take care of Desmond.

The weeks passed by and I began to get into the swing of my new life. I had gone back to work at the bank, and continued with my education at the community college, majoring in marketing. Chris and I tried to work together co-parenting but we often disagreed mostly on visitation. I had no issues with Chris spending time with Desmond, but I wanted to be kept in the loop ahead of time on when he would be taking our son out. Chris felt like he didn't need to communicate ahead of time and would drop in whenever he wanted. To make matters even more complicated his father and mother, Mr. and Mrs. Dixon would likewise take the baby spontaneously, taking advantage of me being at work or school most of the day.

I confronted my parents about needing to be in the loop and how unfair it was to come home from work or school to find my baby randomly gone.

"Now calm down, Peaches," my mother would say. "It's not like we sent Desmond off with strangers. Chris is his daddy and their family won't let anything happen to him. You shouldn't be keeping Chris away from his son."

"That isn't the point!" I would fight back. "I should know beforehand when they want to come and get him! All they have to do is call the day before and let me know! It is so rude to not include me as his mother!"

It never did any good. My parents didn't see it that way and continued to let Chris and his family take the baby whenever they wanted unannounced.

One fall afternoon I sat in the living room looking out the window, waiting for Desmond and his grandparents to return. It had been a long day, and I was frustrated because I had planned to take my son to visit a girlfriend after work. But once again I came home to find the baby gone with his grandparents. While waiting I went through the newspaper classified ads looking for a used car. Chris and I had discussed going in together on one because his car was on its last leg and we both needed wheels without relying on our parents, friends, or public transportation. I had circled a few promising leads when the Dixons pulled up to the front of the house and parked. I put the paper aside and went to open the front door. I had tried to ask Chris' parents to be courteous and give some notice before coming, but they treated me with a certain coldness that I didn't understand.

I opened the door and greeted the Dixons as they came into the living room. Mrs. Dixon said hello and began to tell me how their visit had gone. Mr. Dixon was silent as usual and rarely ever gave me eye contact. Desmond began to cry as he woke up, bringing my mother from her bedroom.

"He must be hungry," she said after greeting everyone. "I'll fix a bottle for him," and off she went to the kitchen.

"I'll help you," Mrs. Dixon offered and picked up the baby and followed mom to the kitchen.

I was about to join them in the kitchen when Mr. Dixon cleared his throat.

"I wanted to talk to you about something," he motioned for me to come closer to the corner of the living room where he stood. I was surprised because this was the first time he had tried to have any kind of communication with me. Maybe he was warming up to me, I hoped.

"So, I know what you are up to," he locked eyes with me. I looked at him blankly, completely puzzled at where he was going with that statement. "You caught yourself a good one with my son," he continued in a low steady voice. "Getting knocked up and trapping Chris so he can pay for your life while you sit back and collect all the money. I've seen it happen many times, and I don't appreciate you putting my son in this compromising position since you won't marry him and raise a family the right way."

His words cut like a knife, what he said was completely insulting and none of it was true at all. I stood there with my mouth open, not sure what to say to defend myself. I understood why they were so cold to me now, and why they purposely refused to communicate and keep me in their circle. I felt tears coming to my eyes, realizing that there was nothing I could do to build our relationship. And I wondered if Chris felt the same way. I thought it was mutual that we didn't want to get married, at least that's what he had told me.

Mrs. Dixon and mom returned to the living room with Desmond and a bottle of warm milk. I quickly wiped my eyes and looked back up at Mr. Dixon. He shot me another glare before announcing it was time for them to leave. Mom ushered them to the door and they left. My mom was completely oblivious to what had just occurred, and I should have told her what happened. Instead I kept it to myself, pushed the pain to the side, and tried to use it as motivation to be more independent and work harder at co-parenting with Chris.

Eventually we found a car we both liked, a blue Oldsmobile, that we shared the title on, and tried to work out a driving schedule. Our system worked well for a time, although we were both immature and had a hard time getting along together.

One spring afternoon Chris picked me up from school and dropped me off at home. The house was empty but my dad's car was parked in the driveway on the side of the house. I knew I would probably find him out back of the house in the large garden plot since the weather was nice. I wandered out back and sure enough there he was turning over the dirt so it would be ready for planting seeds.

"Hey dad!" I greeted him.

He looked up and smiled. "Hey Peaches!"

"Is the baby with mom or the Dixons?"

Dad stuck the shovel in the ground and leaned on it. "Desmond is with his grandparents, they came and picked him up a few hours ago. Your mom stepped out for a bit to go to the grocery store. She should be back soon."

I shook my head, dad knew I didn't like them taking the baby whenever they wanted, but he sided with mom.

Dad could see I wasn't pleased and changed the subject. "How did work and school go for you today?"

I told him how my day had gone, and he listened intently, his eyes lighting up as I bragged about being at the top of my class. Our relationship had drastically improved as Dad had grown past his disappointment and warmed up to my motherhood.

My father was at ease where ever he went, but he was especially in his element when out in the garden working in the earth. He had grown up in a family of sharecroppers in the deep south of Alabama. They worked in the cotton fields that they leased from the landowners in exchange for a roof over their heads and sometimes a small amount of money at the end of the harvest. The sharecropping system was designed to take advantage of poor blacks and whites by exploiting them for cheap labor while making it nearly impossible for them to get ahead financially and own their own land.

Despite growing up poor, dad did receive an education, and when he was grown he joined the army. Most of his family still lived in Alabama, as a child we would take trips to visit my relatives who still worked in the cotton fields and cotton mills.

"What do you think about the elections in South Africa?" I asked. Earlier that week South Africa had held its first fully integrated national elections, and Nelson Mandela was elected as the first black president of South Africa.

"That makes me so happy," Dad grinned. "Mandela spent 27 years in prison for fighting for equal rights. It reminds me of Joseph in the Bible. If God is on your side, He will bring you from up from the low place and put you in a place of honor. I was watching all those people line up for miles as far as the eye could see to vote for the first time, some of them were singing and dancing while they waited for hours and hours. It's a beautiful thing."

"Do you think we'll have a black president one day?" I asked.

"I don't think America is ready for that yet. They'll probably elect a woman before a black man. We've come a long way but we still have a ways to go."

As we talked we could hear the distant bells as they chimed from the Dayton National Cemetery down the street.

"We were the first black family to move into this neighborhood," Dad continued, looking around the quiet backyard. "That was back in the early 1950's. As soon as we moved here, a lot of the white people moved out. There were a lot of people who didn't want to live or raise their families around black people. The department stores downtown were segregated, the owners refused to serve us 'coloreds' as we were called back then."

I listened quietly. Dad didn't talk to me much about the racism he experienced in his life. Having grown up in the deep south in the prime of the Klu Klux Klan, he and his siblings had witnessed blatant hatred and discrimination first hand.

"Racism is everywhere," Dad said bluntly. "When I was overseas in the army, fighting in France, my buddy and I were patrolling through this little French village. We noticed these women were following us and staring. We ignored them at first but they kept following and whispering and pointing at us. Finally, we stopped and asked them what they wanted. One of them spoke some English and she asked, 'We are wondering, where are you hiding your tail?' My buddy and I looked at each other knowing what she might be talking about. She continued on giggling as she spoke. 'We were told you were monkeys, and so we have been trying to see if your tails are showing.'"

I had heard this story a few times, and I could always see the pain in my father's eyes as he recounted this experience. I marveled at the strength it took to be able to fight for a country where you were considered a second-rate citizen or even an animal. Whether blatantly in your face like the lynching's in the south, or passive aggressively like moving away from a black family, racism cuts deeply to the soul of the discriminated.

"But no weapon formed against me shall prosper," dad smiled, looking directly at me. I could see that his faith in God had given him inward strength to stand and not be torn apart by self-hatred and bitterness. "If God be for us, who can stand against us?"

"Amen," I smiled back at him and wrapped my arms around him in an embrace.

"So, Peaches," my dad had a twinkle in his eye looking down at me. "I can count on you to help me out in the garden this year, right?"

I smiled. Dad knew I was way too busy between work, school, and taking care of Desmond to be of any real help in the garden. "I don't think you want my help. You know I don't have the green thumb you and mom have. I killed that cactus I had back in college."

Dad threw his head back and laughed. I laughed along with him.

Mom pulled into the driveway, with a car full of groceries. Dad and I walked over to help her carry them into the house.

"I love you, Agaytha." I could feel the pride in his voice.

"I love you too, Daddy."

It Takes a Village to Raise
A Single Mom
Agaytha Corbin's story

End of the Chapters Scriptures and Thoughts: Chapter (3)
Helper

Definition of helper: a person who helps someone else

In the Biblical term it is the "Holy Spirit"

In Chapter (3) God sent me and my son help. Actually, throughout my journey as a single mother God sent angels in my path that has blessed both my sons and I. My parents were the biggest help with my move, both my pregnancies and finishing college. Both My parents wrapped me with so much love and support. But I also learned about the "Helper" in this period of my life, the Holy Spirit. Pregnancy and the unknown were very scary for me. How was I going to be a mom, especially with no income, no car, and no home of my own. How was I going to take care of my baby boy?

During my first and second pregnancies God sent angels into my life like my best friends in Cincinnati who gave me a baby shower-and my family gave me one in my hometown Dayton. My friends kept me uplifted through the new path I was on to motherhood. Help from my parents took me in and fed me-prayed over me and encouraged me. Desmond's father who stepped up for the OB appointments. My village was forming.

List Positive Help:

(1) _____

(2) _____

(3) _____

(4) _____

List Negative Help:

(1) _____

(2) _____

(3) _____

(4) _____

When I transitioned home, I went back to a childhood church. And let's say some of the members were not so nice helpers. Some have their own negative perceptions of my coming home pregnant. But God can give you people in your path that you have love even when you don't really care to be around them. I also experienced some unsolicited help like opinions that stung while I was already in an emotional struggle. But this negative help made me stronger in the LORD, His Word, and His will for my life and baby's life.

In the Word, Psalms David asked for God's help as he ran from Saul's' threats. David wrote the Book of Psalms seeking God's refuge-His help. David acknowledged God's help and power. David worships with gratefulness for God's help from his enemies.

Scriptures:

Psalms 22:19 KJV
But be not thou fear from me O Lord, O my strength haste thee to help me.
Psalms 28:7
Psalms 27:9
Psalms 38:22
Psalms 54:14
Psalms 63:7

My Help… my help is the LORD!

Question:

Have you become a help to others; paying it forward?

_____

_____

_____

What kind of help has God given you as a parent?

_____

_____

_____

List the people (your villagers) that God guided to help you and how these villagers helped you and or your family:

_____

_____

_____

CHAPTER

"I really like your new place," said my best friend Colette as she looked around my small apartment.

"Well thank you!" I smiled, bouncing Desmond on my hip. "It's not really in the best neighborhood, but it's home." Desmond was two years old and we had moved from my parent's house to a two-bedroom apartment in the Five Oaks neighborhood in north Dayton.

"I know you were glad to get out of your parent's house, girl."

"THEY were glad to get me out of their house," I chuckled. Two years had flown by quickly, especially now that Desmond had learned to walk and with all that energy he was constantly running around the house every chance he had.

I tried to keep up with friends and socialize in my free time, which was pretty infrequent, since I was still working at the bank full time, as well as working on my college credits. I had a small circle of friends that I still kept up with on a consistent basis. Colette was my roommate from college, and she was my son's Godmother. She didn't mind helping me out with babysitting from time to time, plus when he was with her I didn't have to worry about his grandparents intercepting him randomly.

"So, you said this was a dinner party," Colette said excitedly as we sat down on the green sofa. "Who else is coming?"

"I invited Dylan, and he said he was bringing his girlfriend." Dylan Hersh was one of my best friends from middle school. We met in English class in Wilbur Wright Middle School and also shared a history class. In high school we both were at the top of our classes and took advanced placement college credit courses together. He was a member of DATV, the local public access television station, where he introduced me to film production, as well as public speaking and interviewing. I would not have passed my driving test without Dylan. We both graduated from Dunbar High School in the top 15%, and he went to the University of Cincinnati. I was unsure of what direction I was going, but Dylan encouraged me to check out UC. He was right, I loved it there and even though I had to start a quarter later, I jumped right into college life. Dylan was dating Colette, and introduced us to each other.

A friendly knock on the front door drew our attention.

"That must be Dylan," Collette clapped her hands in excitement.

I stood and walked across the living room and opened the door. There he stood towering over me, smiling his friendly, dorky smile, arms outstretched.

"Agaytha Corbin!" he laughed.

"Hey buddy, how you been?" We embraced, at 6'2 he had to lean lower to give me a hug. "And look at Desmond," he stood back and studied my son in my arm. "He has grown so much since I last saw him!" Desmond looked up and smiled, then held out his arms.

"Hey! He remembers you!" I handed him up.

Without skipping a beat Dylan scooped Desmond into his arms, before stepping back and introducing us to his girlfriend, Vivian.

The five of us went inside, and I left them in the living room to check on dinner and get the table set. While arranging the silverware around the table I could hear the happy chatter as everyone caught up on where they were in life and asked about other friends and acquaintances. I looked up and watched for a minute as they interacted. Dylan was possibly the most charismatic person I knew growing up. Even though we were both nerds in middle and high school, we were the cool nerds. We had many friends and got along with both the jocks and geeks. Dylan had black shaggy hair and deep blue eyes, and a smile that could put anyone at ease. He was one of the handful of white people that went to our predominantly black high school. His family lived in east Dayton and he would have gone to Belmont High School, but Dunbar had the best scholastic program at the time.

"Dinner should be ready in about 10 minutes," I announced before joining everyone in the living room.

"Mr. Hollywood was telling us about his new movie he wrote and is currently producing," Colette brought me up to speed on the conversation.

"He's the next Quentin Tarantino," His girlfriend Vivian bragged.

"You always did have a talent for storytelling," I added. "All those television shows you made in high school. They were all really good. Everyone knew to go talk to you if they wanted to be on TV."

"Well, he is much bigger than that now," Vivian interjected. "When his grandfather died, he left Dylan more than enough to move to Los Angeles and start a new professional production company. He is going to do so many bigger things now. Red carpet here we come." She locked her arm in his and gave him the goo-goo eyes.

Colette's eyebrows went up, and she turned to me slowly before we locked eyes. I could tell she was holding back a major eye roll at Dylan's girlfriend. We were both aware of his production company and how well off he had become. A year and a half earlier Dylan had premiered one of his independent films in downtown Dayton at the Neon movie theater. The event was like a class reunion, everyone who was still locally in town as well as some classmates from far away colleges flew in for the weekend to be a part of Dylan's special event. I remember looking around the small crowded lobby and realizing how many people he had connected with in high school. He had given people of all ages a platform to be actors, interviewers, production crew, and he even highlighted local singers, rappers, and musical talent in his public access shows. And in the middle of all the buzz stood Dylan, grinning from ear to ear.

Dylan suddenly seemed self-conscious about all the praise directed his way. "So Agaytha," he deflected. "How have things been with you? How is the family?"

"Everyone is doing well," I looked down at Desmond who was playing with his toys on the living room floor. "My mom and especially dad said to tell you hello."

"Your dad really liked me, especially after driving school," Dylan's face lit up.

"What happened at driving school?" Vivian asked.

"It's a long story," I said, slightly embarrassed. "I could not pass the parallel parking part of the driving test to save my life. My dad tried to teach, Mom coached, nephew Frank tried to help, all my cousins gave it a shot, but I failed over and over again. They all gave up! So here I am senior year of high school, possibly the only one without a driver's license at the whole school. And Dylan had the patience and nerves of steel to get me to the point of passing my drivers' test. And my dad especially will never forget that."

"You were *horrible*," Dylan closed his eyes and shook his head.

"How bad was she?" Colette teased.

"She was so bad that when I picked her up for her first parking lesson her dad took me to the side and told me he would pay for new tires but I was on my own for the bumpers," Dylan joked.

"He was good with you riding the bus or catching rides, but he couldn't afford the insurance on all them cars you crashed into trying to park?" Colette added.

I stood up. "Dinner's ready."

Everyone laughed.

At the dinner table over a meal of salad, spaghetti and meatballs, and garlic bread, we reminisced about old times.

"Now you and Dylan met in middle school, right?" Vivian asked me. "And then you and Dylan met in college?" She looked at Colette.

"Yes, you are right," Colette answered for us. "And then Dylan introduced me to Agaytha and we hit it off so well that we decided to be roommates. And we've been besties ever since."

"That is so cool," Vivian said before sipping on her drink.

"What was it like being friends with Agaytha in middle school?" Colette asked.

"Agaytha has always been cool people," Dylan took a bite of garlic bread and continued. "She is so talented and intelligent. I knew she would be doing big things in life. You wouldn't know it now, but she has a bit of a wild side too."

"Here we go again," I shook my head.

"What do you mean?" Vivian asked.

"Well, her mom and dad were so much older, that everyone thought they were her grandparents," Dylan began. "They were so old school that at times they were kind of out of touch with how things were. Like the time in Jr High you got your mom to take you and your friend to that Prince concert."

Vivian's mouth dropped open. "He is so sexual! I went to his concert last year and had a wonderful time, but my parents would never have let me go while I was that young!"

"Mine either!" Dylan shook his head. "I tried to use the 'all my friends are going' excuse, but they were not having it. I liked Michael Jackson better anyway."

"Mom loved that purple rain song," I explained. "And concerts that they went to were so different back in the day that I guess she assumed that nothing too wild was happening there, so she did drive me and my friend there, and picked us up after it was over."

"You took advantage of that one girl," Colette shot me a look. "Did Prince have on the leather mini vest with seat cut out the pants?"

We all laughed. "It was off the hook, and he had on the purple suit with the platform boots and the frilly blouse for at least half of the show."

"She did the most in Jr High," Dylan continued. "She was always skipping classes and going to the Salem Mall or the Boys and Girls Club."

"What changed for you before college?" Colette asked. "You were always fun and we had good times, but you were more reserved by the time I met you. At the rate you were going it's surprising you didn't have a baby long before now."

"She wasn't a promiscuous girl at all. She was the biggest tomboy in middle school," Dylan pointed out. "You did change though. Right before high school you got serious about your academics and your grades made a U-turn."

I nodded. It was around that time that my favorite aunt, Clara, passed away. Aunt Clara was my mother's older sister, and she always reminded me of a black Audrey Hepburn. She always dressed with such class. Suits fit to a T, beautiful jewelry, and flawless makeup. I always wanted to be like her when I grew up. She taught me how to be a lady, and how to carry myself as a young black girl. When she died, I was determined to stop being rebellious to my parents and to be someone my family and the Lord could take pride in.

"She still had her moments in high school," Dylan went on. "Agaytha and Frank threw the city's most legendary house parties."

"Not the city, just our high school!" I knew with Dylan's knack for storytelling, we were in for some embellishments.

"How many people that didn't go to our school were there?" Dylan looked at me sideways.

"Frank and I had joint birthday parties, and since he went to a different school, yes there were kids from other schools." I explained.

"So you had parties when your parents went out of town?" Vivian asked.

"This is the good part," Dylan was smiling from ear to ear.

"No, my parents were so cool that they let me and Frank have our parties at the house. And they went back into their bedroom, closed the door, and played cards and watched TV. And everyone that came to our party knew there would be no drinking or smoking in the house. Everyone was respectful of our home, so there were never any fights and nobody ever trashed the house."

"Wow, that is awesome," Colette nodded at me.

"It really was," Dylan looked up from twirling his spaghetti. "Frank had the music turned up, everyone was dancing and having a good time. Agaytha had a bowl of punch, cake, and refreshments in the kitchen, and I posted up on the back patio and had the time of my life. There would be little groups of people who would drink or smoke weed in their cars or in the far corner of the backyard. But in high school most of us were not into all that and we just came to party. The last time you had about 60 people come to your birthday party."

"And at midnight, my dad would emerge from the back room and shut the party down. And everyone left respectfully and went on with their night," I passed the garlic bread around the table.

Dylan grabbed another slice. "Your sweet sixteenth birthday got a little rowdy, though." He leaned forward in his chair and whispered, "Someone spiked the punch!"

I laughed, "Yeah, someone did spike the punch that time."

"It was *so good* though," Dylan was laughing too. "Those were the best times. We didn't know how good we had it back then. We didn't know how hard being grown up would be. Not a care in the world, just happily living life." Dylan watched Desmond in his high chair sitting next to me, eating spaghetti with his little hands, getting more sauce on his face than in his mouth. He looked lost deep in thought as he considered the changes in our lives since high school. Next to him, Vivian also looked detached, picking at her nails, as if she was bored because the conversation wasn't revolving around her.

"So, Vivian," I transitioned. "Are you from the Dayton area?"

"No, not really," Vivian perked up. "I'm from Centerville, and all my family live there." Dylan looked slightly embarrassed for a brief second at his girlfriend's bougie statement because in reality Centerville is a suburb of Dayton and very much in the Dayton area. As Vivian went on, Colette's eyebrows slowly raised higher and higher at her "Valley Girl" demeanor which contrasted harshly with Dylan's laid-back ways. After listening for a few minutes Dylan jumped in the conversation.

"How's your love life treating you?" He could probably guess that it was non-existent, but it was nice of him to ask anyway.

"Not as exciting as yours," I paused, because at times it was hard to discuss the difficulties of single parenting without venting or bashing my son's dad for his shortcomings. "I don't really have time for a love life with working full time, going to school, and taking care of my son."

"And how are things with Desmond's dad?" Dylan did have a way of asking the most pointed questions when he wanted. And the truth was that things were going increasingly bad. I suspected that he was stalking me occasionally and a few weeks ago he had called child services on me. On top of that he was not paying any form of child support, leaving the full financial burden of caring for Desmond on my shoulders. It was becoming harder to find the silver lining in our situation.

"We have our struggles," I said slowly.

"Mmmhmm," Colette added. My bestie knew how I felt about bashing my sons' father and covered for me. "You met Chris before, and you know how he can be."

"Yeah we all have our struggles," Dylan sighed.

Vivian gave Dylan a sharp glare, and then abruptly announced, "It was nice finally meeting you all, but we should be going."

Dylan shrugged and shook his head as if this was the standard ending and stood to follow Vivian who was making a beeline for the door. "Thank you so much for your hospitality, Agaytha! Everything was great!"

"We have to do this again sometime soon," I opened my arms for a goodbye hug.

"We definitely do!" Colette laughed. "Don't you go forgetting about us Mr. Hollywood."

Dylan embraced us both and looked over at Desmond who had fallen asleep in his high chair. He gently brushed his hand over Desmond's little head of baby curls and nodded. Vivian stood by the door with her arms crossed and it was obvious she was not on board for hugs.

"Good night ladies," He smiled at us again, opened the front door and with a final glance and wave he followed Vivian out into the night.

Colette closed the door behind them. "WELL!" She said dramatically, "I don't know what Dylan sees in that girl. She doesn't give him much space to breathe."

"She is attractive," I admitted. "And Dylan always has had a big enough heart for anyone."

"You're right, but why is he always out here trying to save these heifers? I don't get it," Colette shook her head and sat down with me on the green sofa. "She acted superior and didn't light up unless she was talking about herself or Dylan's career. I've seen her type before, she doesn't love him and she's probably in it for the money."

"Yeah, that's possible," I said, thinking back to how the talk of Hollywood was all she seemed to care about. The sudden ending of the dinner party had made me feel uneasy. "Thank you for jumping in when Dylan was asking about Chris. I really didn't want to say too much to Dylan or Vivian."

"You know I got your back, girl!"

My hand shook as I pressed rewind on my answering machine. There had to be some kind of explanation because the message I just heard made no sense at all. Dylan was dead, just one short week after our dinner party, he had committed suicide. I pressed play on the answering machine again.

"Hi Agaytha. This is Vivian. I just wanted to let you know that Dylan killed himself yesterday. He put a shotgun in his mouth and blew his head off. I know you were close friends and you would want to know. Okay, Bye."

The turning cassette tape wheels blurred out of focus as tears began to flow from my eyes. This couldn't be true. Dylan had so much promise, so much potential, so much work left to do.

I became aware of Desmond tugging at my black pants suit, looking up at me with concern in his eyes. I sighed, picked him up and walked away from the phone. My brain was spinning with pain, horror, and sadness. I put Desmond down in his playpen and then went to find my address book. I had to call his mother to find out what happened.

I found the book and flipped to the H section. I found Mrs. Hersh's listing, picked up the phone and dialed her number. The phone rang one time before I heard Mrs. Hersh on the other line.

"Hello?"

"Hello Mrs. Hersh?" I took a deep breath and looked up at the ceiling. "This is Agaytha." I stopped. I didn't want to ask, but I had to know if the message was true.

"Oh Agaytha!" His mother's voice shook. "Dylan is gone, his dad and I went to identify him this morning."

"Oh Mrs. Hersh," I began to cry. "I'm so sorry!"

There were not a lot of details to patch the story together. Vivian was the last person to see him alive. She wouldn't say if they had an argument or if he seemed upset. And later that evening Dylan ended his own life, just about a week after we had all had dinner together. Mrs. Hersh had just gotten back from their home in Centerville, after Vivian had called her to come pick up Dylan's belongings that she had put in trash bags out in the driveway. His clothes, cameras, films, and lights were all sitting out next to the street for her to collect.

"I'm so sorry," I cried. "Dylan was one of my greatest friends in the world." I could still see clearly his tall, dorky looking self. His jet-black hair falling into his deep blue eyes as he beamed from ear to ear, smiling down at me in middle school. All the days studying together and academically dominating our high school. His unselfish attitude, and willingness to share his knowledge with anyone. How even without a video camera, he made everyone around him feel like a star. His laid-back demeanor that even won over my dad's respect and admiration. Dylan Hersh truly treated everyone as he would want to be treated and his life shone with a golden light, basking everyone in his warmth.

It Takes a Village to Raise
A Single Mom
Agaytha Corbin's story

End of the Chapters Scriptures and Thoughts: Chapter (4) Distress

The definition of Distress is extreme anxiety, sorrow, or pain. In Biblical terms it is the extreme state of being in great trouble

In Chapter (4) God had me tell the personal story of my childhood friendship with a gentleman who succumbed to his own distress. This portion of my journey was distressful because me and my best friend did not know how traumatized and depressed our friend Dylan was before his suicide. He was a part of my village in the early years. However, I realized that when you are young you tend to be self-centered, busy and a bit detached from some of your village members. You miss the opportunity to pour the love of Jesus Christ to a friend in distress.

In the book of 2 Samuel David experiences the loss of his best friend Jonathan and his mentor King Saul.

Scriptures:

2 Samuel 1:1-26 KJV

And David said unto him, How went the matter? I pray thee, tell me. And he answered, That the people fled from the battle, and many of the people also are fallen and dead; and Saul and Jonathan, his son are dead also. And David said unto the young man that told him, How knowest thou that Saul and Jonathan his son be dead? And the young man that told him said, As I happened by chance upon mount Gilboa, behold, Saul leaned upon his spear; and, lo, the chariots and horsemen followed hard after him. And when he looked behind him, he saw me, and called unto me. And I answered, Here am I. He said unto me again, Stand, I pray thee, upon me, and slay me: for anguish is come upon me, because my life is yet whole in me. So I stood upon him, and slew him, because I was sure that he could not live after that he was fallen: and I took the crown that was upon his head, and the bracelet that was on his arm, and have brought them hither unto my lord. Then David took hold on his clothes, and rent them; and likewise all the men that were with him: And they mourned, and wept, and fasted until even, for Saul, and for Jonathan his son, and for the people of the Lord, and for the house of Israel; because they were fallen by the sword. And he said unto me, Who art thou? And I answered him, I am an Amalekite.

2 Samuel 1:26 KJV

I am distressed for thee, my brother Jonathan: very pleasant hast thou been unto me: thy love to me was wonderful, passing the love of women.

What were some distressed situations that had impacted your life presently and in the past?

Example(s): when a friend or family member turns against you. When you\ have lost something or someone special

(1) _____

(2) _____

(3) _____

How or who helped you get through the distressed situation?

Example(s): David had a strong prayer life; he turned to God. He sought help from the Lord during his loss. David lamented over his friend and mentor's death

(1) _____

(2) _____

(3) _____

Scriptures to pray through when distressed:

1 Samuel 14:24
1 Samuel 28:15
1 Samuel 30:6
2 Samuel 1:26
2 Samuel 22:7
1 Kings 1:29
Psalm 4:1

CHAPTER

FIVE

"Are you ready to go?" Frank, my nephew asked. We were standing in the front yard of my apartment in Five Oaks. We had just finished loading all my belongings into a U-Haul truck and I had taken a breather after locking the front door.

"Yes, I am," I said confidently. "I am ready to leave this chapter behind me." The neighborhood had taken a turn for the worse during the crack epidemic of the early nineties. It was so sad to see the once beautiful neighborhood slowly fall apart as crime skyrocketed. As the number of people addicted to crack grew, so did the home invasions, robberies, and shootings. The last straw for me was about a couple months earlier when I came home from work to find broken glass strewn around the front yard from someone who had tried to break into my home. The slumlord who owned the building refused to do anything to secure his property, and he took his sweet time to replace the broken window.

"Then let's go!" Frank opened the cab door of the truck on the passenger's side. I climbed in and he closed the door behind me. I looked out the window for one last look at the old apartment. Frank climbed in the truck, closed the door and started the engine.

We navigated our way through the maze of barricaded streets. The city of Dayton's solution to the rising crime was to block off access to the inner neighborhoods where crime was the highest. Their reasoning was that by making limited access and adding speed bumps, the slowed flow of traffic would discourage the rampant crime. As far as I could see, the crime remained the same, and all they did was make emergency response difficult and discourage the residents from wanting to live there.

Frank pulled the truck onto Salem Avenue. In the distance at the top of the hill was Good Samaritan Hospital. The all white eight story building was a landmark that could be seen for miles around the Miami valley.

"So how have you been, Auntie?" Frank teased. He was only a year younger than I was so our relationship was more like a brother and sister.

"I am doing better now," I laughed.

"I bet you are Mrs. new homeowner," he joked again. "You gonna have to hook me up with one of them new houses."

"I can get you a mortgage loan for a house at a decent percentage." My new job at the bank was in the mortgage department.

"I just want the house, not the mortgage," Frank chuckled.

"You know that's not how it works," I laughed again.

"Well, congratulations anyway," He grinned over at me. "You are doing big things. Your family is proud of you!" Frank turned the truck on Cornell Drive and we slowly drove down the two-lane street though the neighborhood. "How are things going with little Desmond? The other time I talked to you, the both of you had chickenpox!"

I wanted to laugh, but the colds, flu's, and chickenpox that Desmond picked up from his daycare and passed on to me were no joke. I didn't have chickenpox as a kid and so I had to call off work for a week when he gave it to me.

"Well at least you got some extra time to spend with your son," He remarked. "It was probably more miserable than when you got snowed in together."

"That was way better," I nodded. The blizzard that hit that past winter had brought over a foot of snow overnight, and although it was financially inconvenient to not be at work, it did bring us closer together for a few days. "We did have a good time playing with all the Christmas gifts you guys got for him."

Frank smiled remembering the gifts he had brought over for his little cousin.

"That was a great Christmas! In some ways things are getting better even though the struggle is real in other things. How is your little business going?" Frank was referring to my side hustle, "Beauty Control." Even though I was busy with work, school, and parenting, I made time to diversify my portfolio.

"Beauty Control is going great! I've done a lot of networking and meet a lot of business minded people," I smiled remembering meeting my new best friend, Katrina at an entrepreneur conference during last fall.

Katrina and I had attended the "Beautiful Women We're Talking To You!" conference sponsored by local radio station WROU.92 featuring Dr. Beatrice Berry. At the end of Mrs. Berry's speech, she had asked if there were any questions. The room fell silent until I stood and asked my question. Katrina admired my boldness and approached me at the end of the meeting and from there the two of us had become best friends.

"I'm glad to hear that you are making new connections in your life. How about those dates you went on? Anything serious going on in that department?"

"No," I sighed. "There is nothing serious happening there."

"Really?" He raised his eyebrows. "I thought you went on another date with that one guy."

"WE did," I shook my head. "Him, me, and his mother!"

"What?" Frank exclaimed before beginning to laugh. "Are you serious?"

"Yes! We went on our first date and it went well. He seemed like a nice young man who was very respectable and had potential. Then on our second date he brought his mother to dinner. I didn't mind, eventually I would want to meet her and of course I would want him to meet my parents. But on our third date he brought her again. And to top it off she was very overbearing and she completely dominated the conversation.

So, I decided it was not going to work. I need a man that is there for me, and not attached to his mother at the hip."

"Wow," Frank was at a loss for words, which rarely happened. "So, no more 'Mamma's Boy' for you, huh?"

"I am good. I wish him well, I'm sure there is someone out there for him. But I think he has already found her."

"She's been there from the very beginning," Frank joked. "But seriously, I can see why you didn't want to be the third wheel in that relationship."

"I do hope that there is someone out there for me," I looked out the window at the suburban landscape passing by me.

"I do know someone you may be interested in," my nephew winked at me. "He's a good friend of mine, and actually he's helping us move. You'll meet him at the new house." Frank turned the truck on to Gettysburg Avenue.

"Who is he?" I asked.

"His name is Rod Rodgers," Frank continued. "I've known him since high school, and he's a great guy. And he most definitely is NOT a momma's boy."

"I know Rod, we all would hang out at the University of Cincinnati!" I was dating Chris at the time, but as the social butterfly of the black students on campus I knew most of the prominent fraternity and sorority members. UC was a hub of black social activities, and some of my friends even got to know and date major league Football and Baseball players.

"Those were the days," Frank grinned as we turned onto another side street in a more rural neighborhood. "I forget you were the 'Go to Person' on campus. Matter of fact, you had your own apartment off campus so you could pretty much get away with anything."

"You know I didn't get into any trouble," I reminded him.

"True, you were a good girl, but you knew how to throw an epic house party."

"We had all that practice from the house parties in high school at mom and dad's house." We both sat for a minute, smiling at the happy memories. We were so caught up in reminiscing that we passed our street.

"That was the street," I pointed back.

"I got you," Frank shook his head, clearing the memories and coming back to the present. He turned into the parking lot of the Salvation Army, checked for traffic, and made a U-turn back onto the main street.

We slowed down and turned on to a smaller street in the Townview neighborhood. We passed rows of small ranch style homes with neatly mown yards before pulling up behind my Geo Metro parked out front of my new home.

"Well, at least you are closer to your mom and dad," Frank frowned looking at the slightly run-down appearance of the house.

"It does need some work," I admitted. "But anything is better than that old apartment."

"If you say so," Frank looked doubtful.

We got out of the moving truck and I walked up the sidewalk. I was naïve as a new homeowner in regards to what pitfalls could manifest over time. I fumbled with my keys until I found the house key. Even Frank's suddenly critical mood couldn't bring me down as I opened the screen door and placed the key into the front door lock. I turned the key and opened the door.

"Home sweet home," I said to myself as I entered. I had already brought over smaller loads of my belongings with my car. The bigger furniture I had saved for today. Mom had helped me with packing up the kitchen things. Dad's health was sharply declining. That year he was having a hard time keeping up with the garden he had planted earlier. He still helped with watching Desmond, but when I would look into his eyes, some of the spark had begun to disappear.

"I got the truck open," Frank announced. "Just let me know what furniture you want in which rooms and we'll get you settled."

Frank and I walked the house and I directed where I wanted the furniture to go. As we wrapped up the tour we heard a car horn toot outside.

"That should be Rodney and Fred," Frank grinned, opened the front door and headed outside. Fred was Frank's best friend and Rodney's older brother.

I followed my nephew to the front yard and watched as he shook hands and hugged his buddy Fred and then Rod. Rod looked over at me over Frank's shoulder and smiled at me. His chocolate colored skin contrasted beautifully with his perfect white teeth, and I found myself smiling back at him. He was taller and more muscular than I had remembered from back in college. I was in a relationship back then and I had never really stopped and really checked him out like that until today.

"Hey Agaytha!" His deep-toned voice was inviting as he held out his arms to embrace me. I was completely drawn in as I stepped forward to hug him. Even though he towered over me, I felt a comfort and warmth that I had not felt since my first love back in high school.

"You two have fun," Frank's teasing brought me back to the present. "Fred and I can do all the work."

Rod laughed sheepishly and I slowly let go of his strong arms. "There's more where that came from," he whispered before winking at me.

It took the four of us no time at all to unload the truck and get the furniture situated around the house. During the move Rod had taken off his T-shirt and I was having a hard time not checking out his athletic figure. Later as the guys prepared to leave, I slipped my phone number into Rod's hand.

"Call me?" I asked, looking up at him.

"Definitely," he looked directly into my eyes and flashed that million-dollar smile.

I could still see that smile in my mind's eye later on when my mother came by to bring Desmond to our new home.

"Well, you sure are glowing," My mom noted almost as soon as she saw me.

"I'm just happy to be all moved in," I tried to play it off.

"Uh-huh," she looked over her glasses at me suspiciously. "Moving into a new house don't make a woman glow like that."

"How was Desmond?" I tried to change the subject. We both stood and watched my son as he ran around the new house exploring all the rooms.

"He was active, just like he always is. We went for a few walks and I took him to the park. We might have to look for a different playground. Residence Park is getting a little sketchy with all the people hanging out at that corner store on Edison all the time." Even my parents' neighborhood was feeling the effects of the rise of crack and its influence in the city.

My mom shook her head and then continued. "But Desmond was well behaved. He ate good and took a nap today, he should be ready for bed soon with all the running around he did." My mom shifted over to the kitchen and began opening one of the boxes marked "Glasses." She started unpacking and removing the newspaper from a glass. I grabbed another box of dishes and joined her.

"How is daddy doing?" I turned to look for Desmond. He was in the living room playing with a couple of Hot-Wheel cars. I looked back at mom and noticed the worry lines creasing her forehead.

"He's losing steam," she finally said. "You know your father has been running like a locomotive engine his whole life. Always full speed ahead. But now..." Her voice trailed off. "And it's not just him. I feel it too. We are both getting up there, Peaches." She reached up and put a glass in the cabinet.

I didn't know what to say. I felt a little bad about how much I depended on them to help me with Desmond, even though I know they didn't mind and were happy to help.

"Is there anything I can do to help?"

"You are so helpful," my mom affirmed. "Just being around and giving us a handsome grandbaby to love is enough. Anytime God gives us life and energy to enjoy you both is a blessing from above."

She smiled at me and then walked over to the dining room table, pulled out a chair and sat down. I went over and joined her. She continued to smile as she looked around the room until her eyes caught sight of an unfamiliar T-shirt draped over another one of the dining room chairs. I looked over and realized it belonged to Rod. I looked back at mom and just that quick she put it all together.

"So, Frank did say that he had some friends helping him get you moved today." My mom raised her eyebrows at me. "Maybe one of them got you glowing this evening."

I was so busted.

"Yeah, Frank re-introduced me to Rod." I admitted.

"I see," mom nodded slowly. I fully expected her to launch into a lecture about the dangers of shacking up with the opposite sex.

"Well, it is good to see you in a happy place again," mom continued. "It has been a while. Just be careful, Peaches. You have a family now, and whatever decisions you make in life don't just affect you. They affect the next generation. You ain't in charge no more." My mom motioned to Desmond in the next room. "You have to be intentional about how you live your life, and contentious of the effects that your decisions have on your son."

"I hear you momma," I was almost relieved that the conversation hadn't turned into a long sermon. Growing up in a Christian home, "playing house" or "living in sin" were synonymous for unmarried couples who lived together. It was frowned upon in church circles and to many of the "church mothers," it was the worst of the seven deadly sins. At this point I had not even considered Rod and I living together, but building a relationship was something I felt we could do together.

Over the next few months Rod would find a reason to leave something over during his visits. A tool here or some jeans there. He was a great handyman, and with this house in particular, there always seemed like there was something that needed to be worked on. And Rod was very willing to be of service. When he wasn't over helping or hanging out, we would talk on the phone whenever we had free time. I really liked that he had a great work ethic and he was very motivated and goal oriented. And I was determined that our relationship was going to last. I would give it everything to make it work.

One afternoon I came home from a busy day of work and as I entered the kitchen I stepped into a puddle of water on the floor. Upon further inspection, the pipes connecting to the kitchen sink were leaking. I called Rod and soon he was there, toolbox in hand.

He struck a pose in the doorway. "Somebody called for a plumber," he said in his most sexy voice.

I laughed at his innuendo and showed him where the leak was under the sink. One thing about Rod, he had a great sense of humor and he could always make me laugh. A few minutes later after Rod's inspection there was less to laugh about.

"The pipes under the sink are all rusted out," he began. "When Townview was built in the early 50's they more than likely used galvanized steel or cast iron for the plumbing. Copper is better for plumbing but it's more expensive. I can patch up the leak but eventually you may need a professional to replace everything. And if there is a leak here, there are possibly potential rusty pipes all over the house."

As I mentally did the math for how much everything would eventually cost, my countenance fell. All the hopes I had for making a new start as a homeowner were slowly evaporating. Rod could sense my growing frustration and he drew me into his arms.

"Don't worry Agaytha," He looked down deeply into my eyes. "I'm here for you." He slowly leaned forward and kissed my lips. I kissed him back and we stood there in each other's arms as I felt myself slowly melt away.

Rod's analysis was accurate. Over the next few months additional leaks popped up around the house. And although he made himself available at all hours of the day and night to help me with the issues that seemed to be escalating, eventually all the pipes in the house had to be replaced. In the meantime, Rod began staying overnight occasionally and we started seriously dating.

It did seem like as one part of my life became fulfilling, another part would fall apart. Desmond's dad, Chris couldn't accept that I had moved on with my personal life back when I lived in the Five Oaks neighborhood, and he reported me to social services. He claimed that with all the work that I did that our son was neglected, and he alleged that there was abuse due to occasional cuts and bruises Desmond would get from being a rambunctious boy. Fortunately, the social worker who was assigned to us had common sense, and once she visited and saw for herself the robust Desmond in action, she reported that there was nothing sinister taking place.

Currently Chris took me to court for custody of our son. He claimed he wasn't getting all the time that he wanted to spend, which was entirely untrue.

In the end he was ordered to pay child support, and was awarded with a standard visitation order, which less than he had with complete access before. It wasn't enough for him though, and for some reason at this time he started stalking me from afar at work and home. Eventually my brothers, Frank Jr, Bennie, and nephew Frank III, had to confront him in person about his erratic behavior. Whatever they said to him in their "come to Jesus" conference finally set him straight and there was peace.

I was still struggling financially from all the court costs, the daycare expenses, plus the mortgage and homeowner pitfalls, and a couple of predatory loans, all while working full time and working on my marketing and management degrees. I had graduated from Sinclair Community College and I had transferred to Wilberforce University in Xenia, Ohio. Rod was my rock through the tough times and in my mind, it began to make sense that if we lived together, there would be so many positive effects.

We would save so much money in living costs, we would save in gas money, everything would be so much more efficient. We were already sleeping together, so whether we shacked up or not, that was not going to change any time soon.

So, I asked Rod to move in, and he agreed and we began life together. At first there was so much that was working for us, that I felt it was meant to be. I was so blinded by my love for him that I couldn't see myself falling into darkness. I was living in rebellion to what God had stated in his Word. My mother took immediate concern and wrote me a letter, pouring out her heart. She reminded me how I was raised with Christian values and how my lifestyle was in direct conflict with those morals. She had noticed that my church attendance was slacking, which possibly had more to do with Chris and his family who still attended our family's church. But her concern was more about where I was with my relationship with the Lord. She begged me to slow down and that in seeking God and his righteousness first everything else would fall into place. I took note of her concerns, but I was too determined to play the wifey role and make Rod into my husband and I continued on my mission.

After my mother shared her concerns, I noticed red flags began to pop up. Rod had a lot of friends and I was open to them all hanging out at cookouts and playing cards in our home. I even joined them in the card games sometimes, unless they were playing spades. Spades was the Corbin family card game that was taken very seriously. I knew how to play, but on one occasion at a family reunion as a teenager I lost the game for our team. In a rare moment in the heat of the competition my dad lost all his cool and yelled at me for the mistake I made. I was completely traumatized and never played spades again, mainly because it was one of the few times I knew I had completely disappointed my father.

Rod and his friend could be competitive at times, but the red flags for me were that with the social activities came drinking. I didn't mind the occasional drinking, but I started to notice that Rod would drink every day. And even though he was not abusive, I began to worry that he was an alcoholic.

As time progressed the house started to have other problems. My dream home was becoming a nightmare. Once the interior pipes had all been replaced, then the septic pipes acted up. The toilet would back up, and the sink drains would clog. In addition, the roof had started to leak.

The stress from all my problems began to have an effect. I started feeling sick to my stomach at random times throughout the day.

I shared my issues with my best friend Katrina about how things were going at one of her visits to my house of calamity. We had found a lot in common in our entrepreneurial interests after meeting at the conference. She was working with AmeriCorp, but had her own beauty product side business. She also had a daughter right around Desmond's age. We were sitting together on my bed talking in my room while her daughter, and Desmond hung out playing in the front of the house. After telling her about all my homeowner woes and some of the ongoing problems I was having, her reaction surprised me.

"It's amazing how the most intelligent people get remedial over the simplest things," she remarked.

I stared at her blankly, expecting an explanation for what she meant.

Katrina stared back at me. "We doing this? Okay, let me break it down. You should take a pregnancy test."

I had not even considered this possibility of myself being pregnant, but it did make sense. I ran out to the local pharmacy and bought two pregnancy tests. A little while later Katrina and I sat in my bedroom hovering over the sticks waiting for the results. A few minutes later the results showed. I was pregnant again.

It Takes a Village to Raise
A Single Mom
Agaytha Corbin's story

End of the Chapters Scriptures and Thoughts: Chapter (5) Movement

The definition of Movement is an act of changing physical location or position or of having this changed. A change or development. A change of place or position or posture.

In this chapter I tell of a move that I did for me and for my son's safety. In reality, since my college days as a young adult, I was a restless soul, the free-spirited thinker, always on the move. Then came motherhood, I had to look at the needs and safety of another human being who needed me. So, I moved in this motherhood life trying to do my best in covering my son's needs. I also began a movement of dealing with my past and present pain. Even in movement with my second child, I realize now that constant movement kept me from truly healing, dealing and coming to terms to some trauma. GOD is the guide to movement. He sent His son who left us with the Holy Spirit, who helps in my movements. In movement GOD created earth and the season. He gave light in the darkness.

Scripture

Genesis 1:2-3 NIV

2 The earth was without form, and void; and darkness was on the face of the deep. And the Spirit of God was hovering over the face of the waters. 3 Then God said, "Let there be light"; and there was light.

In the Book of Genesis GOD told His story of creating earth and man-and then He commanded man to move around the earth that He made. He commanded man to move about and multiply the earth.

What is God guiding you to move on in your life?

_____

_____

_____

What happened in your life because of an unplanned move?

_____

_____

_____

How did you get through a traumatic move? What kind of go to God things did you do to get through the move?

_____

_____

_____

In your prayers, are you asking God to give you direction in your next move? And if so what are some of those moves (ministry, love life, family and career)?

_____

_____

_____

As a single mother with two sons, I often wonder how I get through the many moving parts of my life. And the answer always lands on God's hand on my back pushing me and holding my hand while I plunge into motherhood. In telling my story I encourage others to move on from being broken to being made whole in Christ Jesus. He moved in my life so smoothly and so strongly that I still know it had to do with the move of a living God. He kept me and my village!

Scriptures on Movement:

Psalm 18:36 NIV. You enlarge my steps under me, And my feet have not slipped

Proverbs 30:19 NIV. The way of an eagle in the sky, The way of a serpent on a rock, The way of a ship in the middle of the sea, And the way of a man with a maid.

Matthew 9:19 NIV. Jesus got up and began to follow him, and so did His disciples.

Exodus 14:19 NIV. The angel of God, who had been going before the camp of Israel, moved and went behind them; and the pillar of cloud moved from before them and stood behind them.

Psalm 18:28 NIV. For You light my lamp; The LORD my God illumines my darkness.

Colossians 1:23 NIV. If indeed you continue in the faith firmly established and steadfast, and not moved away from the hope of the gospel that you have heard, which was proclaimed in all creation under heaven, and of which I, Paul, was made a minister.

CHAPTER

The twilight of the setting sun flooded through the open blinds of our new home as I unpacked another box in our spacious kitchen. We had moved yet again to a ranch style house in an adjacent neighborhood because the problems at the old house kept multiplying. The last straw for us was when the roof had begun to partially collapse and a swarm of bees started nesting in the eaves of the disintegrating house.

Rod and I worked together in silence. We were both glad to be out of the money pit house, however our relationship was still in a rocky place. We had so many issues that we needed to work through, and I was beginning to realize that my mother was right when she told me that Rod was not ready to be in a serious relationship.

"Did you go see your dad today?" Rod asked, flattening and folding an empty box.

"Yeah," I looked up at Rod. The light from the window basked his handsome mahogany profile in a golden glow. "He's doing better since they moved him from the Veteran Affairs Hospital to the Good Samaritan Hospital."

Both of my parent's health had taken a turn for the worse. My father's kidneys were failing and my mother was recovering from hip surgery. They both were in the hospital concurrently and to share the responsibility of their care I had taken power of attorney for my dad and my brother, Frank Jr, had power of attorney for my mom. At the same time, I juggled my relationship, caring for my son Desmond, a full-time banking career in management with a new company, a side hustle as a beauty consultant with my best friend Katrina, and pushing through school for my Bachelor's degree. I was literally running two households physically and financially as I cared for my parents and I worked to keep up with life.

A few times a week I would visit for a couple hours with my father. I was seven months pregnant and it was very noticeable. My dad would always tease me when I went to see him. "When are you gonna have that baby?" he would ask with a big smile. I would laugh, and we would chat about life and what was going on in the world.

"Well at least he is getting good care and he got out of the VA hospital," Rod remarked. Back then the health care that the VA provided was notoriously horrible because the military hospitals were grossly underfunded.

I nodded and watched as he opened the refrigerator and reached for a beer. I didn't mind him drinking, but these days it seemed like it was growing even more frequent than before. I knew we both were busy with work, but it seemed like outside of work and drinking, he would either be hanging out with his friends or sleeping. Regardless of my concerns, I continued to do my best homemaking and wifely duties, even though we still weren't married. I was determined to prove everyone wrong about us and have my way "happily ever after" with the man I loved.

As the twilight slowly faded away and the shadows of the evening engulfed the world outside, I drew the curtains and tidied up the kitchen. Rod was in the next room going through more boxes and watching television. The telephone rang and I answered. It was my older brother Frank. We had to keep in contact frequently to coordinate details of helping with our parents' care. Mom was bouncing back considerably well after her surgery, but Dad seemed to be in a consistent decline. We discussed what options we had for his care, we had talked before about putting him in a nursing home where he could have constant medical attention. Frank mentioned some of the nursing homes he had checked into. There were quite a few that were a definite pass for us due to their notoriously awful track record with their patients. We had narrowed our search down to a couple of nursing homes in the Trotwood area. Frank and I went back and forth discussing the pros and cons of the locations, visitations, and most importantly the health care Dad would receive. We finally decided on Englewood Manor and made the arrangements to have him moved there.

A few months later I made my way through the maze of hallways in the nursing home on another one of my almost daily visits to my father. I was very pregnant at this time, and once again I had toxemia which added to the swelling in my legs and feet.

As I waddled into my dad's nursing home room I immediately sensed something was different. I looked over at my dad and smiled, waiting for his usual "When are you gonna have that baby?" Instead my dad stiffened and looked towards the window. My heart sank and a lump grew in my throat.

"Daddy!" I grabbed his hand, sat in the chair next to him and tried to get him to look me in my eye. "Are you okay?"

He wouldn't reply or acknowledge me, instead he continued to look in the direction of the window. My gaze followed to the window. There was nothing special about what he could see from his hospital bed, just the clear blue sky. I looked back at him. All of the sparkle in his eyes was completely gone. The tears started to trickle down my face as I realized my father was facing the end of his life. I reached my arms around him and held him close. He hugged me back and we embraced for a few moments as I tried to hold back the waterfall of tears that wanted to flow.

"How are we doing today Mr. Corbin?" The afternoon shift nurse asked. My dad pulled back and looked towards the nurse.

"I'm doing okay," he replied.

The nurse went through her routine and my dad answered her questions. I held his hand and kept looking for eye contact. My dad continued to avert direct eye contact throughout our time together. My brother Frank and my mother also stopped in and he didn't look at my mother either. We visited for a while, Frank and my mom kept trying to engage him in conversation and lighten the mood.

I sat there silently, holding his hand and searching for the right words to say. All

I could say was, "I love you Daddy." I could feel his love, although inaudibly in those moments, the warmth of his love never wavered. I had always been a daddy's girl, from the beginning until now. Like the biblical father Abraham, I was the miracle daughter of his old age, his pride and joy. The bright glow of my father's love had always been a constant source of nurturing light, like the sun. There were only a couple of times in my entire life where his disappointment in me had eclipsed that sunshine. I realized as I saw my dad fading that he, Ralph Corbin, was refusing to say goodbye. He didn't want to go. But his time was closing in on him.

That night I lay alone in bed, unable to get comfortable. Rod wasn't at work, but he hadn't come home either. It was typical behavior for him, and I was so tired and busy with other things that I didn't make a big deal of it. Sometimes he said he was out hanging with friends, or out drinking, and other times he wouldn't bother with an explanation.

I adjusted the pillows under my swollen feet and leaned back again in bed. Desmond was sleeping soundly in his own room, but sleep eluded me. The telephone on the nightstand next to me rang. I almost hesitated to answer, I had a feeling that it was someone with bad news. I went ahead and answered, and it was the nursing home calling to inform me that my father had passed away a few minutes before.

The next few days were a blur with funeral arrangements, phone calls, with family and friends stopping by to check on me and mom. I was beginning to see how one sided my relationship with Rod truly was, because during those difficult days he was completely unavailable mentally and physically. He didn't even go with me to my father's funeral.

"I'm worried about you, Agaytha," my mother took my hand in hers. "How are you doing?" My mother was heartbroken and grieving the loss of the love of her life.

"I'm okay," I replied. At this point being okay was the most cheerful way of saying that I was surviving. There was so much pressure and stress that I felt multiplied by the hormonal roller coaster of being pregnant. I truly was unable to completely even acknowledge the extent of my broken heart in those moments because of all the responsibilities I felt compelled to fulfill.

We were standing in the front of the family's home church with my brothers next to my father's casket. The sanctuary was completely packed with family from Alabama, church members, friends, co-workers, and others who had known Ralph Corbin and also felt the loss of one of the pillars of the community. So deep was the feeling, that even the church mothers left their judgmental sentiments about my living in sin and being unmarried with a child yet again behind them, and genuinely embraced me in their support of our family.

The military friends and co-workers from Wright-Patterson Air Force base were well represented. During my father's time abroad, fighting for his country in World War II, he had gained the admiration of his fellow soldiers, both black and white. And many of them who were still living made their way to his funeral to give their final respects to a true American hero.

Much of the church was full of its own members who had taken time off work during that week to be a part of this homegoing service for one of the pillars of the congregation. Both my father and mother had been active members of the church for decades. Their humble lives together had been a shining light, from leading in Bible studies, to their work in foster care, to their personal interactions showed people what the love of Jesus could do in a Christian family.

Many of daddy's foster kids were present, but by far the majority of the people in the church filled to capacity were dad's family from Alabama. He was from a large family of brothers and sisters who remained as sharecroppers, and although dad had found his path in life in distant Ohio, family reunion time always centered around his birthday on July 1st back home in the South. During those summer days around Independence Day we would reunite nearly every year to celebrate the family as well as the life of one of its foundational members. And now his village had returned to say goodbye to "Uncle Ralph," as he was known to the rest of the generation my age. Although everyone in that room was feeling the pain of loss, we grieved together in the quiet strength of unity that Ralph Corbin had left with us.

In that quiet strength I found comfort as the funeral proceeded. It was my task to give my father's Eulogy. It had taken many days of reflection and a few hours of fact checking amongst the remaining Corbin siblings and my mother, but I stood before the congregation and retold the story of my father's life. But the cold hard facts about Ralph didn't cover the essence of who he was to the ocean of sad faces clad in black that crowded that Midwestern church. So, at the end of the Eulogy of my dad's life, I shared a poem I had written about my father, telling the spectrum of my feelings towards the man that had given us all everything in return for so little. I stood before the church in such strength that I made it all the way through my remarks without completely breaking down.

I rode in strength with my mother and close family in the black limousine in the long procession of cars that lead the village in our pilgrimage from Englewood to West Dayton.

I sat in strength with my mother and brothers, Frank and Bennie, at the Dayton National Cemetery, though dad's internment service. I held my mother's hand as we listened to the rifle salute, and taps played on the trumpet, and we looked over the casket draped in the American flag at the sea of white tombstones in the background.

My mother cried through the majority of the church and military services. She was also a pillar of strength, but life had taught her how to be strong and also know and express herself emotionally.

There were many tears that flowed from my eyes that day, but I dared not to give way to the multitude of emotions that I felt. My older brothers had become the new pillars of the village, and my stoic demeanor reflected that I too was prepared to be one of those pillars.

But Angerlener Corbin could see through the strong walls I was trying to seal myself into. "Peaches," she whispered with tears in her eyes. "Are you really okay?"

It Takes a Village to Raise
A Single Mom
Agaytha Corbin's story

End of the Chapters Scriptures and Thoughts: Chapter (6) Father "ABBA"

The definition of a Father

Of a man cause a pregnancy resulting in the birth of a child. Is a protector, a teacher and an encourager; a person who picks you up when you fall, brushed you off and lets you try again; admired and much loved; often referred to as a son's first hero and daughter's first love.

Mark 14:36 NIV. And He said, "Abba, Father, all things are possible for You. Take this cup away from Me; nevertheless, not what I will, but what You will."

This is one of the chapters of my story that tells how my parents really truly were the start of my village. My early father Ralph Corbin was a true dad. He taught me to be a strong young lady. My earthly father was the first gentleman introduced into my life. He made me feel like the little lady even in my wrong. He covered my mother and I like we were his treasures. I was a true "daddy's girl". My mother always told the stories to family and friends on how I could get my dad to do most things that she couldn't. When I was in bed at home as a child, I could hear my parents talk and play cards, argue and laugh with one another. When I heard my father return home, I felt safe and secure in our home. My earthly father was worried about my pregnancy while he was here, and he always looked out for me and my son Desmond. As my parents aged and got ill, it became a privilege to take care of my dad. Because he had done so much for me as his daughter. When my dad passed away, it gutted my heart and yet I still had to be a mother and a mother to be while working. Grief had manifested into my own health and wellness. And this is another miraculous move from my Heavenly Abba. I needed to lean in on the everlasting arms of Abba during this loss and during the high-risk pregnancy. As I walk with Christ I'm learning in His Word that God wants us to call Him Abba, Our Father. He loves us despite who we are and what we do. Like my early father Abba has kept me safe and secure daily. Jesus Christ His Son called Him Abba in the Garden of Gethsemane. In Jesus's darkest moment He prayed and humbled himself to Abba for help.

Mark 14:32-35 NIV. Then they came to a place which was named Gethsemane; and He said to His disciples, "Sit here while I pray."

33 And He took Peter, James, and John with Him, and He began to be troubled and deeply distressed.

34 Then He said to them, "My soul is exceedingly sorrowful, even to death. Stay here and watch." He went a little farther, and fell on the ground, and prayed that if it were possible, the hour might pass from Him.

36 And He said, "Abba, Father, all things are possible for You. Take this cup away from Me; nevertheless, not what I will, but what You will.

Abba showed me love and comfort during the death of my dad. I realized that I hid in work and in everyone else's pain and did not really deal with the pain and trauma. But God kept me as I tried to be a mom and a provider.

Fathers wrap their arms around their children; they are the protectors. And Abba was definitely my protector as I tried to get through both my high-risk pregnancies. I lost an important person in my village. And it changed the course of my adult life in every way.

How has your earthly father impacted your life?

_____

_____

_____

_____

If you did not grow up with your earthly father, what male person has impacted your life-your village?

_____

_____

_____

_____

How has the Heavenly Abba helped you in your darkest hour?

_____

_____

_____

_____

Give thanks to the Abba for His:

_____

_____

_____

_____

Scriptures:

Proverbs 1:8 NIV "Hear, my son, your father's instruction, and forsake not your mother's teaching."

2 Corinthians 6:18 NIV "And I will be a father to you, and you shall be sons and daughters to me, says the Lord Almighty."

Psalm 103:13 NIV "As a father has compassion on his children, so the Lord has compassion on those who fear Him."

Proverbs 22:6 NIV "Start children off on the way they should go, and even when they are old they will not turn from it."

2 Samuel 7:14-15 NIV "I will be a father to him, and he will be a son to me. When he does wrong, I'll discipline him in the usual ways, the pitfalls and obstacles of this mortal life. But I'll never remove my gracious love from him."

Proverbs 23:22 NIV "Listen to your father, who gave you life, and do not despise your mother when she is old."

Proverbs 23:24 NIV "The father of a righteous child has great joy; a man who fathers a wise son rejoices in him."

Psalm 32:7-8 NIV "You are my hiding place; you will protect me from trouble and surround me with songs of Deliverance."

Proverbs 4:11-12 NIV "I will guide you in the way of wisdom and I will lead you in upright paths. When you walk, your steps will not be hampered, and when you run, you will not stumble."

Luke 15:20 NIV "But while he was still a long way off, his father saw him and was filled with compassion for him; he ran to his son, threw his arms around him and kissed him."

Deuteronomy 1:31 NIV "There you saw how the Lord your God carried you, as a father carries his son, all the way you went until you reached this place"

Hebrews 12:7 NIV "Endure hardship as discipline; God is treating you as sons. For what son is not disciplined by his father?"

CHAPTER

SEVEN

I was not okay.

As I lay in my bed staring at the ceiling I waited in the dark for the alarm clock to go off. It had been one week since my dad's funeral service. Once again, I was alone in my bed, wishing I had someone I could talk to and process all of the pain and sadness I was experiencing. The mental agony almost eclipsed the physical suffering I felt in my bloated, pregnant body.

I was back to work at the bank. They had given me some time off because of my father's death, but today was yet another day of the work grind. I really didn't mind going back to work because it gave me something to do and focus on. It was a welcome distraction from the gaping emptiness that was left in my daily schedule of visiting my dad in the nursing home.

The alarm clock began its screeching and was instantly silenced as I sat up to officially begin the day. In my condition sometimes, I wondered why I even set the alarm every night. Sleep was a rare luxury, and setting an alarm to awaken me was wistful thinking most nights because of my pregnancy.

I woke up Desmond and prepared breakfast for us while trying to tidy up around the house in case Rod came home at some point during the day. My son was too young for kindergarten, but I had enrolled him in an early education program instead of daycare, and I felt like even in his rambunctiousness they were doing a good job teaching him instead of just babysitting.

I sat down with him and we had breakfast. I had our routine down to a science. We still had a few minutes to finish getting ready to walk out the door. For a moment I considered what it would be like to have an extra pair of manly hands around assisting me in my morning routine, but the reality of doing it all alone was becoming more and more evident.

It was an overcast dreary day. I was wearing my favorite maternity blue power suit. After dropping Desmond off at his stop, I drove out to Centerville where I had an early meeting with a mortgage client. The couple were both doctors and I was showing them an expensive mansion. During the meeting the husband and wife kept looking at me in a strange way. I was used to getting looks from people sometimes because of how pregnant I was, but this was different. The wife especially looked like she wanted to say something, but in the end, they kept it all business and we closed our deal.

I did feel slightly off as I walked to my car, and got into it. I couldn't get my vision to focus. I took my time for a little while trying to shake the blurriness, but in the end, I drove away and tried to work around my visual impairment. Eventually I ended up lost, driving around the maze of upper-class suburban homes, looking for a familiar landmark or street that could re-orient me to where I was located.

Once I figured out where I was, I had lost quite a bit of time, so I stopped by a friend's house to take a quick break before heading back to work. Lisa was a lifesaver, especially when I was working south of town and needed a pit-stop in my pregnant condition.

"Oh, my goodness, Agaytha!" Lisa exclaimed when she opened the door. "Come in, girl!" Her face showed concern as she helped me into the house and tried to get me comfortable on her living room sofa. "You don't look too good. You look like you need to go to the hospital."

"I'm okay," I smiled up at her. I honestly did feel better being there with her at her home.

We caught up for a few minutes on news and life, all the while I could tell Lisa was analyzing my condition.

"Well you caught me before lunch, so you should join me," Lisa offered. I accepted her invitation. After a couple of sandwiches, I did feel a lot better, and my vision had somewhat returned to normal. Lisa was hesitant about me leaving. She still felt like I needed to go to a hospital, but I was determined to push my way through my work day to the very end.

Back at work, I checked my schedule. I had one more mortgage client left for the day. By this time my vision had worsened from blurry to double vision. I was starting to worry about these symptoms I was experiencing, so I called my mother. After our conversation she was very much ready to call an ambulance for me, but I persuaded her to hold off until I finished with my clients for the day.

I closed my eyes and laid my head down on my desk. "Help me Lord," I prayed inwardly.

"Agaytha, are you good?"

I raised my head up from the desk. One of the bank tellers was standing in the doorway of my cubicle. We locked eyes and her face went from concerned to alarmed. "You look like you need to go to the hospital!" she said, and moved towards the phone on my desk.

"No," I put my hand over the phone. "I am okay, it's just normal pregnancy stuff. I just need a few minutes and I'll be fine."

The teller didn't look like she believed me at all. She stepped back and adjusted her glasses back on her face. "Your clients are here," the teller announced. "I can have them see another loan officer."

"Go ahead and send them in," I gathered myself together and gave the best smile I could muster.

The teller backed away and blurred into the background. I gathered the loan paperwork together and was about to make sure I had everything together when I noticed out of the corner of my eye that the teller had pulled aside one of the branch managers and was talking to him while looking in my direction. Before I could react, a couple appeared in my doorway.

"Come on in," I said in my friendliest voice. As I focused on their faces I was surprised that I recognized them. It was "Mama's Boy" as nephew Frank had dubbed him. We had gone on a few dates but never hit it off. And with him, no surprise, was of course his mother. As they sat down and made themselves comfortable, I scanned through the paperwork and realized that "Mama's Boy" and his mother were applying for a mortgage together. Evidently whatever they had was working, and they were going into a joint business venture together. They were relatively cordial, they did remember me and "Mama's boy" even wished me congratulations on my apparent pregnancy. The irony of seeing them again helped me focus and I helped them get their final loan paperwork approved and send them on their way.

After they left, a wave of nauseousness took over and I threw up in my office waste basket. Afterward I leaned back in my chair and tried to center myself as the room spun around me. A few minutes later my boss appeared. One look at me up close and she was ready to call the ambulance to take me to the hospital.

My work village had been very supportive during my entire pregnancy. They had even thrown a baby shower for me a few weeks ago! If I ever needed some time off work, they accommodated me with no complications. Although my co-workers' concerns were mounting, I was determined to walk out of my job with my own two swollen feet.

And so within a few minutes I found myself alone in my own car in the underground bank parking lot. I could feel my blood pulsing through my veins. It was a sensation that I had almost gotten used to over the past few weeks, but today it was especially pronounced. As I gripped the steering wheel, I noticed that I couldn't feel anything in my right hand. It was completely nub. I started to feel an urgency to make it to my gynecologist.

I eased out of the parking lot onto the street, and turned on my windshield wipers because the incoming rain made my already compromised vision even worse. In addition to the blurred and double vision, I was beginning to see black spots. I sat for a moment to focus, and then pulled into traffic. The route was familiar, I had driven it hundreds of times which helped considering my impairment. I pulled onto Monument street, and headed towards north Dayton.

I remembered my dad. "When are you gonna have that baby?" he was always asking. Thinking of him teasing me made me smile. I missed him so much. It made me so sad to think that he would not get to meet the grandbaby he had looked forward to seeing. I wiped tears from my eyes as I drove across the Monument street bridge.

The future seemed very uncertain. I knew that eventually my parents would pass away, but I could never imagine a future without them in it. I would miss seeing the look of pride in my father's eyes as he watched his new grandkids grow. I had always hoped that my dad would be there to walk me down the aisle when I got married to Rod. And he and my mother would be at peace knowing me and my children were going to be cared for in life by a man who truly loved us and would do anything for us.

As I turned onto Salem Avenue the future stretched in front of me and all I could see was a black hole of shattered dreams and unfulfilled hopes. Ultimately I would lose my mother too, and it would be just me and my kids alone against the world. I blinked because the black spots in my vision were starting to dominate the picture as I peered into the windshield blurred with rain.

A green light in front of me changed from yellow to red, and I slowed to a stop. I looked to the left and my eyes focused on the sign in front of the United Way building and a pair of outstretched hands cupped together. I remembered a Bible verse I had learned in Sunday school. "But Zion said, 'The LORD has forsaken me, and my LORD has forgotten me.' Can a woman forget her sucking child, that she should not have compassion on the son of her womb? Yea, they may forget, yet I will not forget thee. Behold I have graven thee upon the palms of my hands; thy walls are continually before me." Isaiah 49: 14-16 KJV.

The darkness that I felt closing in on me lifted. As I was reminded that God was with me and was holding me in his hands, I could hear God's voice encouraging me in my sadness that I was, and would never be completely alone.

The light changed from red to green and I pulled forward. The black spots still obstructed my vision, but I knew I was going to make it. My heavenly father has the whole world in his hands. His eye is on the sparrow, so I know he watches me too. In the far distance I could see a white light. Somehow the storm I was driving though had missed Good Samaritan hospital, and the skies above it were shinning down on the white building at the top of the hill, making it almost radiate in the glow of the sun.

Within a few minutes I had progressed the couple of miles from downtown Dayton, up Salem Avenue and to my OBGYN, which was right around the corner from the hospital.

After checking in and the usual questions the nurse checked my blood pressure. She began to redden and she looked up at me.

"How did you get here?"

"I drove."

"She drove." Her face turned an even deeper shade of beet red. "I'll be right back," The nurse shook her head and disappeared from the room, quickly reappearing with a doctor. They went over my blood pressure and the doctor looked up in alarm. "She drove here," the nurse added, which added to the look of panic in the doctor's eyes.

He did remain calm however as he came over to me and announced, "We are admitting you to the hospital."

Minutes later I was being wheeled through the emergency room and ushered into a room in the Intensive Care Unit. There was a continuous buzz of people in and out of my room. After sharing my personal information, my mother, nephew Frank, and Rod were notified and the nurses wheeled in an ultrasound machine. They worked in a frenzy while speaking in hushed tones. After a few minutes a doctor came over to me and held my hand.

"Miss Corbin," he began in a measuredly calm tone. "We are facing some complications from your preeclampsia. Your blood pressure is so high right now that it is a miracle that you haven't had a stroke and died today. If you had waited one more hour to come in, it very likely would have been fatal for you and the baby."

The gravity of my situation began to sink in. I was so focused on staying busy and pushing forward instead of listening to the people who were telling me to slow down. My actions could have very well jeopardized mine and my baby's life. Laying there in the hospital I finally had no choice but to rest.

The days slowly passed by. Rod's family, the Rodgers, came frequently. This was to be their first grandbaby and they were very excited to welcome the new life into the family. They even helped my mom with babysitting my son Desmond. Rod came a couple times, mostly with his family. Mom took care of Desmond and brought him by to see me quite a few times. My rambunctious son was excited that he was soon to be a big brother.

My brothers, nephew Frank, Katrina, Colette, and Lisa brightened my time with lighthearted jokes and laughter. Colette even took it upon herself to go to my house and create a nursery for me. They all knew how close to death I had come, and how high risk my pregnancy continued to be as the doctors monitored our condition.

The bank supervisor even looked out for me by making sure all my deals got processed and closed. She came to the hospital and told me that everything was handled and not to stress about my job. My village was growing, but amidst all the support I was still scared.

On the third day the doctors decided to perform cesarean surgery because the baby's heartbeat remained so faint that they couldn't detect it at times. His father, Rod, was there with me when I had the procedure.

My son Lamon Rodgers came into the world on August 11th 1998. He was born prematurely by 7 weeks, weighing 3 and a half pounds. My health slowly improved, and Lamon was a fighter and he pulled all through the intensive care he received.

"You finally had that baby," my mother said with a smile. There was still sadness in her eyes as she remembered her late husband's favorite greeting for his Peaches. "How are you doing, Peaches?"

Tears welled up in my eyes even as I smiled at her. "I am getting better." I was trying to be more open with my emotions, even though at times I was unsure of how to identify what I was feeling. "I miss Daddy."

"I know," mom looked into my eyes and wiped a tear from her own. "I miss him too." She reached for my hand and held it tightly. We sat there silently for a few minutes, lost in the memories of Ralph Corbin and wishing he was there with us.

Mom sighed and then looked at me very seriously. "And what did I tell you that morning you called me before work?"

My mind went back to a few days before. I had forgotten that I had called my mother and talked to her briefly before charging full speed ahead. "You asked me again if I was okay, and told me to go to the hospital and get some rest." If I had heeded her advice I may not have come so close to death's door.

"But you are so stubborn, Agaytha," she gently scolded. "The Good Lord has been looking out for you for sure. It's like that Bible verse you like so much. Psalms 27:5 KJV. 'For in the time of trouble he shall hide me in his pavilion: in the secret of his tabernacle shall he hide me; he shall set me up upon a rock.'"

I nodded and a smile slowly eased across my face. There was much to be uncertain about in my life at that moment, my relationship with Rod still was not on the level I needed it to be for us to consider getting married. My son Lamon lay in an incubator in another part of the hospital, slowly growing to term. Desmond was getting older and getting closer to a place where his dad and I would have to choose a place for him to get a good education. I myself had not yet completed my Bachelor's degree, and even though my career was thriving, I sensed that God had something else in store for me.

I still felt a level of apprehension at the thought of raising two black boys into manhood with the way the world is, but I also felt that God would continue to hide all of us in his secret place. My village was being built on The Rock, and although I could see the storm clouds gathering on the horizon, I knew we would stand tall against the coming tempest.

It Takes a Village to Raise
A Single Mom
Agaytha Corbin's story

End of the Chapters Scriptures and Thoughts: Chapter (7)
Safe

The definition of Safe is protected from or not exposed to danger or risk; not likely to be harmed or lost-free from harm or risk: unhurt

Psalms 27:5 KJV For in the time of trouble He shall hide me in His pavilion; In the secret place of His tabernacle He shall hide me; He shall set me high upon a rock.

I was safe in His arms during the high risk birth of my second child. Safe in my working and dealing with grief. Safe in a relationship that I was hoping would grow into a true committed one. Safe with raising my rambunctious and smart toddler son Desmond. Safe as I made dangerous decisions in getting to the birth of my son Lamon. During my single motherhood life there is a verse or better yet a whole chapter in the Book of Psalms that truly speaks to God's safety net for me. in Psalms 27 David was running from his enemies and from death. David was God's most beloved. He made so many foolish decisions but always worshiped God. David trusted God for his life; he sought safety in God's presence.

Psalms 27:2-3 When the wicked came against me To eat up my flesh, My enemies and foes, They stumbled and fell.

3 Though an army may encamp against me, My heart shall not fear; Though war may rise against me, In this I will be confident.

The village that Elohim was creating for me and for my sons was becoming a safe haven.

What situation did occur where God kept you safe?

_____

_____

_____

_____

How did God create a safe haven for you?

_____

_____

_____

_____

Write down moments in your childhood to adulthood where you felt safe (ex. family, home, community and church)?

_____

_____

_____

_____

Scripture

A Psalm of David. 27 KJV

The LORD is my light and my salvation; Whom shall I fear? The LORD is the strength of my life; Of whom shall I be afraid? 2 When the wicked came against me To eat up my flesh, My enemies and foes, They stumbled and fell. 3 Though an army may encamp against me, My heart shall not fear; Though war may rise against me, In this I will be confident. 4 One thing I have desired of the LORD, That I will seek: That I may dwell in the house of the LORD All the days of my life, To behold the beauty of the LORD, And to inquire in His temple. 5 For in the time of trouble He shall hide me in His pavilion; In the secret place of His tabernacle He shall hide me; He shall set me high upon a rock. 6 And now my head shall be lifted up above my enemies all around me; Therefore I will offer sacrifices of joy in His tabernacle; I will sing, yes, I will sing praises to the LORD. 7 Hear, O LORD, when I cry with my voice! Have mercy also upon me, and answer me. 8 When You said, "Seek My face," My heart said to You, "Your face, LORD, I will seek." 9 Do not hide Your face from me; Do not turn Your servant away in anger; You have been my help; Do not leave me nor forsake me, O God of my salvation. 10 When my father and my mother forsake me, Then the LORD will take care of me. 11 Teach me Your way, O LORD, And lead me in a smooth path, because of my enemies. 12 Do not deliver me to the will of my adversaries; For false witnesses have risen against me, And such as breathe out violence. 13 I would have lost heart, unless I had believed That I would see the goodness of the LORD In the land of the living. 14 Wait on the LORD; Be of good courage, And He shall strengthen your heart; Wait, I say, on the LORD!

Something Called Love.....................

The kind of Love I long for seems so far from me-for my natural
eyes cannot see it! The kind of love I long for is held neither in
the natural but in the Supernatural realm-its something that man
cannot manufacture-nor something I can make-up for myself.
Love is sometimes a mystery-It cannot be packaged. It is sometimes
difficult to let go-and sometimes hard to accept.
Love is "Honest and Healthy"
Love is Compassion toward others, even when they do not Love you!
Love is holding your kids close-hearing them and accepting them for
whom God created them to be. Love is not blind-It "opens" up your eyes
to Life and allows you to go through it with Passion and Courage.
Love is sacrifice of one's self when it's necessary not forsaking
one's Love for Christ; But, showing it even when it hurts!
Love is a cool and wonderful breath of fresh air! I want to breathe again
the sweet odor of Love, the wind of Peace and the breeze of Charity! I
wish to pour out Love like sweet heavy hyssop covering the heads of my
loved ones and healing the wounds of my enemies! (1 John 3:16)

So Jesus, please show Your daughter how to give and receive that kind of Love!

By, Ms. Agaytha B Corbin- A Lover of Christ! 9/30/2007

AGAYTHA B. CORBIN
AUTHOR & BUSINESS WOMAN

A free spirited Lover of Christ who is a strong single mother to two amazing young men; Desmond Dixon and Lamon Rogers. Agaytha is the product of a late in life birth (a Sarah and Abraham baby). A Daddy's Girl." She is the youngest and only the daughter of the late Ralph and Angerlener Corbin. She was raised and educated in Dayton Ohio, where her parents were retirees from civil service at an Ohio Air Force base. She is a passionate servant-leader in her community. Agaytha is best described as a loyal and fierce friend, who takes the time out to listen to her family and friends who share their hopes and dreams. Her family knows her by the nickname "Peaches," a name her late Grandmother gave birth to because she thought that she looked like a round pretty peach.

Agaytha loves to spend time with her sons, family and friends. She travels and never meets a stranger. Agaytha is a compassionate woman who loves Bible Study-learning God's Word is the key to her maintaining her sanity as a daughter to elderly parents, a single mother and a servant leader. She is currently a small business owner and a podcaster. She is a graduate of Paul Lawrence Dunbar H.S class of 88, attended the University of Cincinnati and a college graduate (B.S) of Wilberforce University. Education was and is her super power. And the Church was a place of grace and growth.

Entrepreneurship is in her genes. Her late grandmother and great grandmother were Black business women in Texas and Oklahoma. Her mother taught her to be an independent and smart Black young lady. Drilled in with good work ethics as a kid but at the same time spoiled by being the last child and the only girl. Growing up she witnessed Black business growth and thriving neighborhoods. But by the time she returned home as a mother she witnessed the demise for her former neighborhood and city. And that is when the real journey God placed her on began, for both her and her sons.

She was the President & CEO of the Community Development Corporation Resource Consortium (CDCRC) and has made her mark in the Dayton area as a community development consultant, community-based educator and trainer. Agaytha has developed a stellar reputation for being a pioneer in the Mortgage Industry. During her 15 years of work in the banking industry, Agaytha developed and managed the Dayton area Emerging Market (low-moderate income housing market) Office for two major financial institutions. She holds several business, state certifications. Agatha worked on two national Presidential campaigns in 2007 and in 2012. Ms. Corbin became an important political organizer for the Dayton/Montgomery area. Seeing the disparity not only in minority homeownership, but also in access to capital for small businesses, limited resources for small grassroots agencies and the many emerging predatory lending practices overtaking her community, she became the principal driving force behind the Community Development Corporation Resource Consortium (CDCRC) whose vision is to become a community-based vehicle providing collaborative opportunities that will leverage community resources, create platforms for economic change, increase capacity for non-profit organizations and strengthen micro-enterprise development opportunities in underserved areas.

As the President and CEO of the CDCRC, she has jointly facilitated the development of the Dayton Area Community Grant Center and is co-founder of the Dayton Area Small Business Roundtable Monthly Business Forum Series. As a Community-based educator teaching Financial Literacy to low-moderate income residents is one of her greatest passions. She has just recently taken her passion to another level through the development of a new financial literacy program; "Creating Community Wealth." The principles of utilizing homeownership as a foundation for wealth creation, guarding yourself against predatory lending practices, using micro-enterprise development as a wealth-building tool, understanding and protecting your credit and your assets are taught through this community-based education program.

Presently Agaytha owns her own communication consulting company and travel agency division. Speaking Grace LLC was her long term dream and vision for her future self after her sons became men. Speaking Grace LLC was created because communication was and is a gift for Agaytha and she wants to share and serve clients who wish to expand their communication skills and projects. Running this business is what she loves and wishes to do in her latter days. She learned that if you are working in the field that you love then it will not seem like a job but a lifestyle and God has gifted you with.

Printed in the United States
by Baker & Taylor Publisher Services